NIKON P950 USER GUIDE

A Comprehensive Guide to Mastering Your Superzoom
Camera for Capturing Stunning Photos and Videos

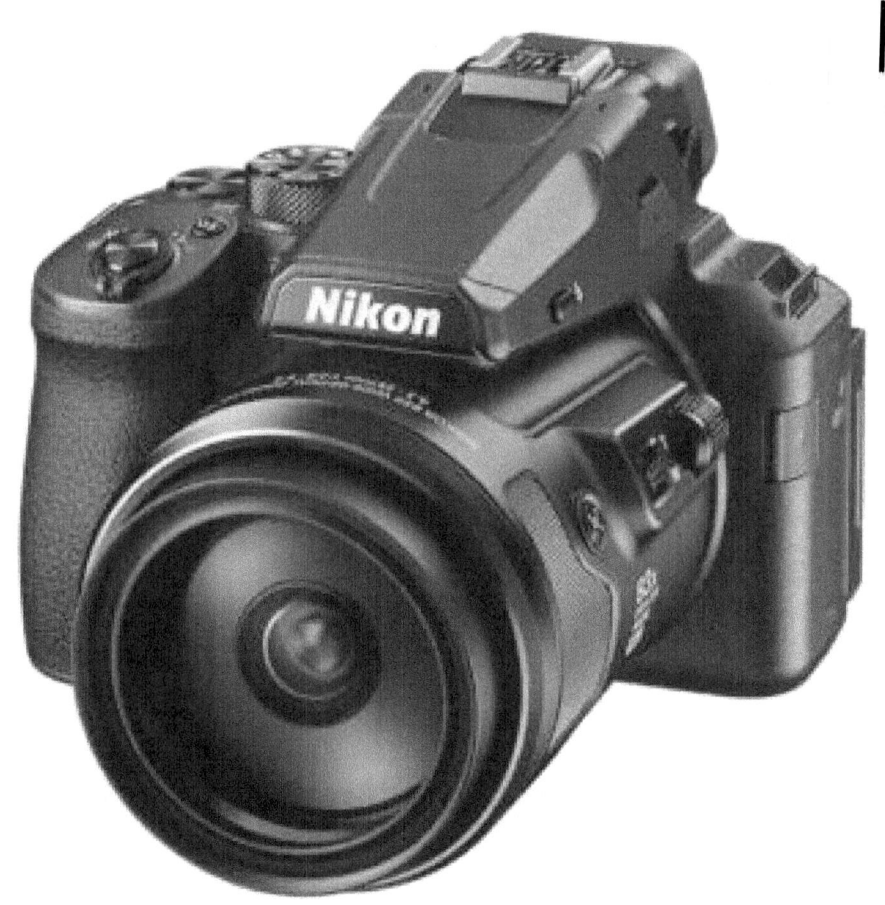

PHILLIP R. DITCH

Copyright © 2024 Phillip R. Ditch

Unauthorized reproduction, distribution, or transmission of any part of this publication in any form or by any means, including photocopying, recording, or other electronic or mechanical methods, without the prior written permission of the publisher, is prohibited.
Brief quotations may be used in critical reviews and other non-commercial uses permitted by copyright law, provided proper attribution is given.

TABLE OF CONTENTS

DISCLAIMER 4
CHAPTER ONE 6
INTRODUCTION 6
CHAPTER TWO 12
GETTING STARTED 12
CHAPTER THREE 20
BASIC OPERATIONS 20
CHAPTER FOUR 32
SHOOTING MODES 32
CHAPTER FIVE 46
ADVANCED PHOTOGRAPHY SETTINGS 46
CHAPTER SIX 60
VIDEO RECORDING 60
CHAPTER SEVEN 70
MENU NAVIGATION 70
CHAPTER EIGHT 82
PLAYBACK AND EDITING 82
CHAPTER NINE 88
CONNECTIVITY 88
CHAPTER TEN 94
ACCESSORIES AND EXTERNAL FEATURES 94
CHAPTER ELEVEN 98
MAINTENANCE AND TROUBLESHOOTING 98
CHAPTER TWELVE 102
SPECIFICATION 102

DISCLAIMER

The contents of this book are provided for informational and entertainment purposes only. The author and publisher do not make any representations or warranties regarding the accuracy, applicability, completeness, or suitability of the contents for any purpose.

The information in this book is based on the author's personal experiences, research, and opinions, and should not be considered a substitute for professional advice. Readers are advised to consult appropriate professionals regarding their specific situations.

The author and publisher are not liable for any loss, injury, or damage allegedly arising from the information or suggestions in this book. Any reliance on such information is at the reader's own risk.

The inclusion of third-party resources, websites, or references does not imply endorsement or responsibility for their content or services.

Readers are encouraged to use their own discretion and judgment when applying the information or recommendations in this book to their own lives.

All rights reserved. No part of this book may be reproduced, distributed, or transmitted in any form or by any means without the prior written permission of the publisher, except for brief quotations in critical reviews and certain other non-commercial uses permitted by copyright law.

Thank you for reading and understanding this disclaimer

CHAPTER ONE
INTRODUCTION

1.1 About the Nikon P950

The Nikon P950 is a high-performance digital camera designed for enthusiasts and those looking for versatility and quality in a compact form. It features a 83x optical zoom lens with a focal length range equivalent to 24-2000mm, allowing users to capture a wide range of subjects, from wide landscapes to distant wildlife.

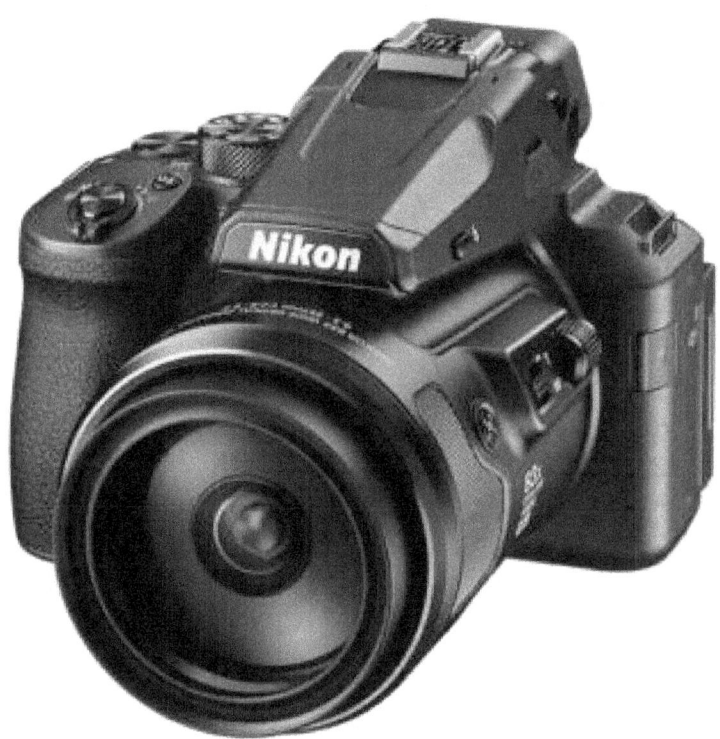

The Nikon P950 is part of Nikon's Coolpix series and is designed for users who need a powerful zoom without the complexity of interchangeable lenses. It combines high magnification with advanced imaging technology to provide excellent image quality and ease of use.

2. Key Features:

- **83x Optical Zoom**: A remarkable zoom range that covers from 24mm wide-angle to 2000mm super-telephoto, making it ideal for wildlife, sports, and long-distance photography.

- **16 MP CMOS Sensor**: Provides high-quality images with good low-light performance, ideal for both stills and video.

- **4K UHD Video Recording**: Capture videos in stunning 4K resolution, along with Full HD and slow-motion options.

- **Vibration Reduction (VR)**: Built-in image stabilization helps reduce blur from camera shake, especially at long focal lengths.
- **Dual Detect Optical VR**: The combination of lens-shift and electronic VR helps stabilize the image even in shaky conditions.
- **SnapBridge Connectivity**: Easily share images and videos with compatible smartphones or tablets via Wi-Fi or Bluetooth.
- **Time-Lapse and Birdwatching Mode**: These special modes are tailored to capture specific types of photography, such as animals in motion or stunning slow-motion time-lapse footage.
- **Manual Control (P/S/A/M Modes)**: Advanced users can take full control over exposure settings (shutter speed, aperture, ISO), providing flexibility for creative shots.
- **Electronic Viewfinder (EVF)**: A high-resolution 2.36-million-dot EVF offers a clear and detailed view for composing images, even in bright sunlight.

3. Design and Build:

- **Compact and Lightweight**: Despite the powerful zoom, the P950 is relatively compact for its class, making it portable and convenient for travel.
- **Ergonomically Designed Grip**: A comfortable grip makes it easier to hold the camera steady for long shooting sessions, especially with the extended zoom.
- **Articulating LCD Screen**: The 3-inch vari-angle LCD screen can be tilted or rotated to shoot from various angles, ideal for selfies, vlogging, or shooting in tight spaces.

4. Performance:

The Nikon P950 is well-suited for both amateur and semi-professional photographers. Its autofocus system is fast and reliable, even when zoomed in, ensuring sharp focus on subjects at various distances. The camera also performs well in low light conditions, thanks to its sensor and VR technology, which minimizes the need for a tripod in many situations.

5. Ideal Use Cases:

- **Wildlife and Bird Photography**: The super-telephoto zoom is perfect for capturing distant animals or birds without disturbing them.
- **Sports Photography**: With its powerful zoom and quick focus, it's ideal for action shots, even at a distance.
- **Travel and Landscape Photography**: The wide-angle setting is great for landscapes, while the telephoto zoom helps you capture subjects that are far away, such as mountain peaks or architectural details.
- **Vlogging and Video Creation**: The 4K video recording capability and the vari-angle screen make it a solid choice for content creators who want a camera with great zoom and video features.

1.2 Box Contents

When you purchase the Nikon P950, the box typically contains the following items:

1. **Nikon P950 Camera**: The main camera body, which includes the built-in 83x optical zoom lens.

2. **EN-EL20a Rechargeable Lithium-Ion Battery**: A battery designed for the P950, providing power for shooting photos and videos.

3. **EH-73P Charging AC Adapter**: The wall adapter used to charge the camera's battery. It comes with a power cord for connecting to an electrical outlet.

4. **UC-E21 USB Cable**: A cable for connecting the camera to a computer or other devices for data transfer or charging.

5. **Lens Cap (LC-67) and Strap**: The lens cap helps protect the lens from dust and scratches when not in use, and the strap helps to carry the camera comfortably.

6. **Viewfinder Eye Cup**: An eye cup for the camera's electronic viewfinder (EVF) to ensure a clear view when composing images.

7. **Quick Start Guide**: A concise guide to help you get started quickly, covering the basics of the camera's operation.

8. **Warranty Card**: A warranty card providing details about the warranty coverage and how to register the product.

9. **Reference Manual (CD)**: The full user manual may be provided in digital format on a CD for more in-depth instructions on using the camera.

10. **Accessories/Software**: Depending on the region or retailer, the box may also contain software or links to software for editing and managing your photos and videos, such as Nikon's ViewNX-i software.

These items should be included in the box, but it's always good to double-check with the retailer if you purchase from a third party.

1.3 Safety Precautions

When using the Nikon P950, it's important to follow the safety precautions to avoid damage to the camera and ensure safe operation. Below are the key safety guidelines:

1. Handling the Camera

- **Avoid Rough Handling**: Do not drop or bump the camera. Always handle the camera with care, especially the lens and screen, to avoid damage.

- **Keep the Lens Cap On**: When not in use, keep the lens cap on to protect the lens from scratches, dust, and dirt.

- **Use a Strap**: Always use the provided strap to carry the camera around your neck or wrist to prevent accidental drops.

2. Battery Safety

- **Use Only Compatible Batteries**: Always use the provided or Nikon-approved EN-EL20a battery. Do not use unauthorized third-party batteries as they may cause damage or pose a safety risk.

- **Avoid Overcharging**: When charging, always unplug the camera once the battery is fully charged to avoid overcharging, which can damage the battery over time.

- **Do Not Expose to Heat or Fire**: Never expose the battery to extreme heat, fire, or direct sunlight, as this could cause it to overheat, leak, or explode.

- **Store the Battery Properly**: When not in use for an extended period, remove the battery from the camera and store it in a cool, dry place.

3. Power Supply

- **Use Only the Supplied AC Adapter**: Only use the supplied EH-73P charging adapter for charging the battery. Using an incompatible charger could cause electrical issues or fire hazards.

- **Turn Off the Camera When Not in Use**: Turn off the camera when it is not being used to prevent unnecessary battery drain and avoid potential overheating.

4. Preventing Electric Shock and Damage

- **Avoid Moisture**: Never expose the camera to water, rain, or high humidity. Moisture can damage the camera's internal components and lead to electric shock or malfunction.

- **Avoid Sudden Temperature Changes**: Do not move the camera directly from a hot to a cold environment, or vice versa. This can cause condensation inside the camera, potentially damaging internal components.

- **Keep Away from Strong Magnetic Fields**: Do not place the camera near strong magnetic fields, such as those from a microwave or speakers, as it can interfere with the camera's functioning.

5. Lens and Screen Care

- **Avoid Touching the Lens**: Do not touch the lens glass with your fingers, as oils and dirt from your skin can damage the lens and affect image quality.

- **Clean the Lens Carefully**: Use a soft, dry cloth to clean the lens. If necessary, use a lens cleaning solution recommended by Nikon and a lens cleaning brush.

- **Avoid Direct Sunlight**: Never point the camera directly at the sun, as this can damage the lens or internal sensor. It can also cause image distortion and potential harm to your eyes when using the viewfinder.

6. Memory Card and Data Safety

- **Use High-Quality Memory Cards**: Always use compatible, high-quality SD or SDHC memory cards recommended by Nikon to prevent data corruption.

- **Do Not Remove the Memory Card During Operation**: Avoid removing the memory card while the camera is reading or writing data, as this may corrupt the data or damage the card.

7. Environmental Considerations

- **Avoid Extreme Temperatures**: The Nikon P950 is designed to operate in moderate temperature ranges. Avoid using the camera in extremely hot or cold conditions.
- **Store in a Dry Place**: Store the camera in a dry, cool location when not in use. Avoid leaving it in places prone to excessive moisture or extreme temperatures, such as in a car on a hot day.

8. General Safety

- **Do Not Disassemble the Camera**: Never attempt to disassemble or modify the camera yourself. If repair or service is needed, take the camera to a qualified Nikon service centre.
- **Be Mindful of Your Surroundings**: When using the camera in potentially dangerous environments (e.g., near water, cliffs, or wildlife), always stay aware of your surroundings to avoid accidents.

By following these safety precautions, you can help prolong the life of your Nikon P950 and ensure safe and effective use of the camera.

CHAPTER TWO
GETTING STARTED

2.1 Camera Parts and Components

The Nikon P950 is designed with various buttons, dials, and ports to ensure ease of use while delivering high-quality imaging. Here's an overview of the main components of the camera:

1. Front View

- **Lens (83x Optical Zoom Lens)**: The large zoom lens offers a focal length range of 24-2000mm (equivalent), allowing for wide-angle to super-telephoto shots. The lens includes a zoom ring for smooth adjustments.

- **Flash**: A built-in pop-up flash for low-light conditions, which can be manually popped up when needed.

- **Microphone**: A built-in microphone for recording sound when shooting videos.

- **Lens Release Button**: Used for removing the lens cap.

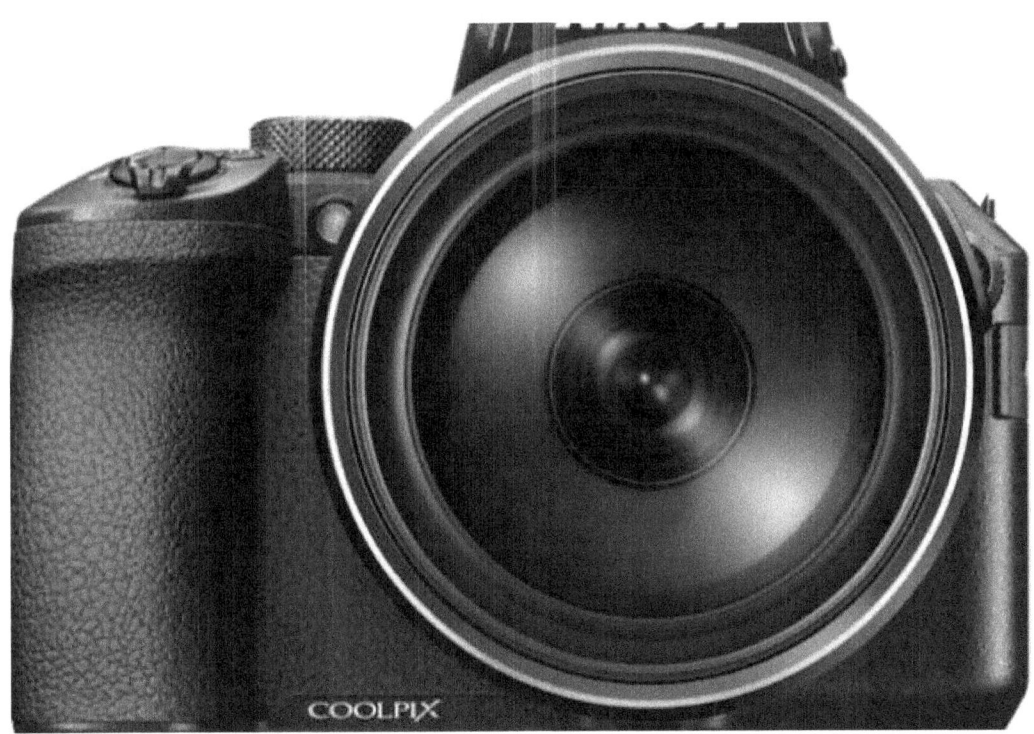

2. Rear View

- **LCD Screen (3-inch Vari-Angle Display)**: A fully articulated LCD screen that can be tilted or rotated to various angles for comfortable shooting and viewing. It allows for selfies, vlogging, and shooting from high or low angles.

- **Electronic Viewfinder (EVF)**: A high-resolution viewfinder (2.36 million dots) located above the LCD screen for composing images in bright light conditions, or when you prefer to use a traditional viewfinder.

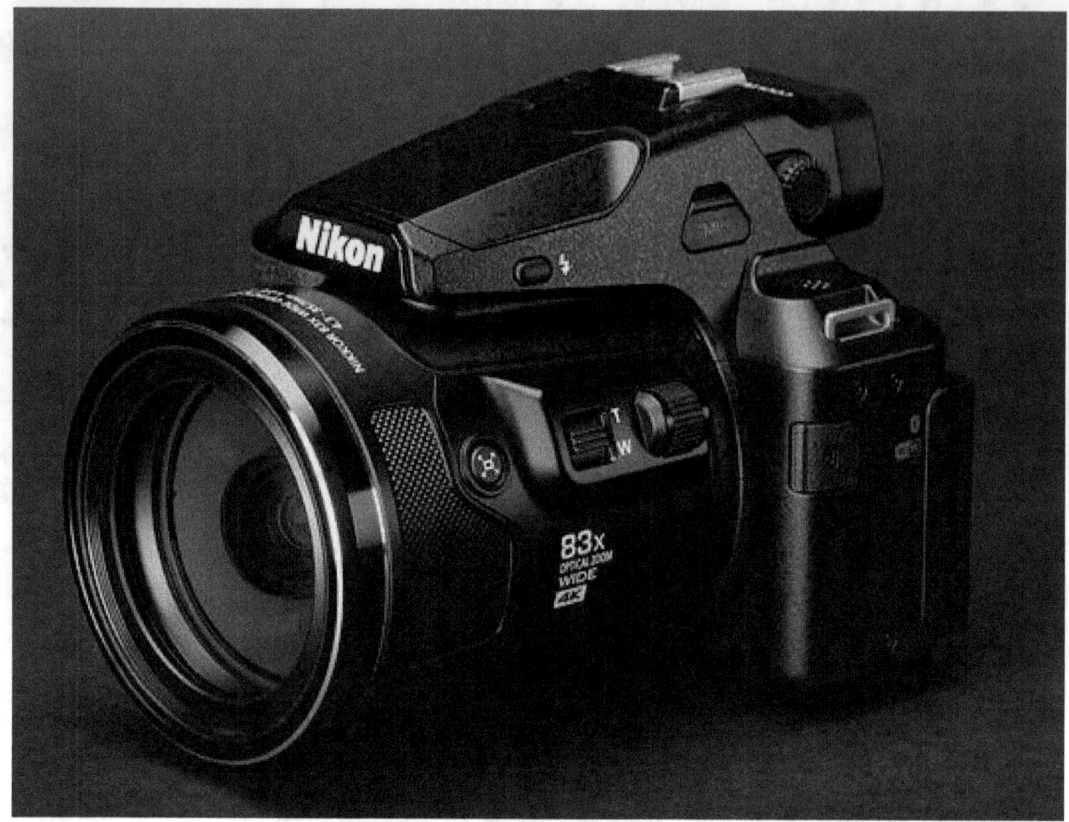

- **Mode Dial**: A rotating dial on the top of the camera to switch between shooting modes such as Auto, Program, Scene, Aperture Priority, Shutter Priority, Manual, and more.

- **Playback Button**: Press to view your captured images and videos.

- **Menu Button**: Opens the camera's menu system to adjust settings.

- **Multi-Selector (Joystick)**: A 4-way joystick for navigating through menus, adjusting settings, and selecting focus points.

- **OK Button**: Confirms selected options or settings in the menu.

- **Delete Button**: Deletes selected images or videos from the memory card.

- **Zoom Control**: Positioned on the back near the shutter button, this control allows you to zoom in and out during photo or video capture.

- **Function (Fn) Button**: A customizable button that can be set to perform specific tasks, such as adjusting ISO or white balance.

- **Battery and Memory Card Compartment**: A slot on the bottom or side for inserting the battery and memory card.

3. Top View

- **Shutter Button**: Located on the right side of the top, it allows you to take photos when pressed halfway (for focusing) or fully (for capturing).

- **Power Button**: Located near the shutter button to power the camera on and off.

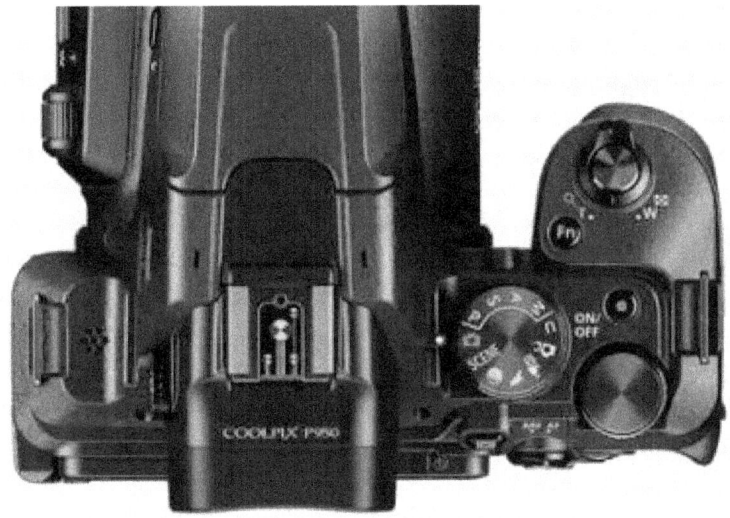

- **Zoom Control**: On the top right of the camera for adjusting the zoom, it allows you to extend and retract the lens.
- **Hot Shoe (for External Flash)**: A connection point for attaching an external flash or other compatible accessories.

4. Side View

- **External Mic Jack**: A port for connecting an external microphone to improve audio quality when recording video.
- **USB/HDMI Port**: For connecting the camera to a computer, TV, or other devices for file transfers or live video output.
- **Tripod Socket**: A standard 1/4-inch threaded socket at the bottom of the camera for mounting the camera on a tripod or other support equipment.

5. Bottom View

- **Battery Compartment**: Houses the EN-EL20a rechargeable battery.
- **Memory Card Slot**: Accepts SD, SDHC, or SDXC memory cards for storing images and videos.

6. Lens Cap

- **Lens Cap (LC-67)**: A protective cover for the lens to prevent damage and dust accumulation when the camera is not in use.

2.2 Charging the Battery

Charging the EN-EL20a rechargeable lithium-ion battery that powers the Nikon P950 is simple, but it's important to follow the correct procedure to ensure safe and efficient charging. Here's how to charge the battery:

1. Charging the Battery Using the AC Adapter (EH-73P)

Step-by-Step Instructions:

1. **Remove the Battery from the Camera**:
    - Open the battery compartment located on the bottom of the camera.
    - Slide the battery lock and gently remove the EN-EL20a battery from its compartment.

2. **Connect the AC Adapter to the Battery Charger**:
    - Plug the EH-73P AC adapter into a power outlet.
    - Connect the small end of the adapter to the battery charger (if provided separately) or directly to the camera, depending on the model you purchased.

3. **Insert the Battery into the Charger**:
    - Place the EN-EL20a battery into the charger, aligning it correctly according to the charging contacts.

4. **Charging Indicator**:
    - The charging indicator light will turn **orange** when the battery is charging and will turn **green** once the battery is fully charged.
    - Typically, a full charge will take around 2.5 hours, but this may vary depending on the charger and battery condition.

5. **Complete the Charging Process**:
    - Once the indicator turns green, the battery is fully charged and ready for use.
    - Remove the battery from the charger and return it to the camera's battery compartment.

2. Charging the Battery in the Camera (Using USB)

If you prefer to charge the battery directly inside the camera, you can do so by using a USB cable:

1. **Turn Off the Camera**:
    - Ensure that the camera is turned off before beginning the charging process.

2. **Connect the USB Cable**:
    - Plug the small end of the provided UC-E21 USB cable into the camera's USB port (located on the side of the camera).
    - Plug the other end of the cable into a USB power source, such as a laptop, computer, or USB adapter connected to an electrical outlet.

3. **Charging Indicator on the Camera**:
    - The camera's battery icon will display a charging symbol while the battery is charging.
    - The indicator will show a full charge when the battery is completely charged.

Note: Charging through the camera may take longer than using the external charger.

3. Charging Precautions

- **Do Not Overcharge**: Unplug the battery once it's fully charged to avoid overheating or damage to the battery.

- **Use Proper Equipment**: Always use the original or Nikon-approved charger and cables to prevent electrical issues.

- **Charge in a Safe Location**: Always charge the battery in a dry, well-ventilated area, away from extreme temperatures or moisture.

2.3 Inserting the Battery and Memory Card

To begin using your Nikon P950, you need to insert the battery and memory card into their respective slots. Here's how to do it:

1. Inserting the Battery

- **Locate the Battery Compartment**:
    - On the bottom of the camera, you'll find the **battery compartment**. There is a small latch that you need to slide to open it.

- **Insert the Battery**:
    - Insert the **EN-EL20a battery** into the compartment, aligning the battery's terminals with the corresponding contacts inside the camera.
    - Make sure the battery is seated securely and fits into place without forcing it.

- **Close the Compartment**:
    - Once the battery is inserted, gently close the battery compartment cover, ensuring that it clicks securely into place.

2. Inserting the Memory Card

- **Locate the Memory Card Slot**:
    - The memory card slot is typically located just next to the battery compartment. You will see a small **SD card slot** (compatible with SD, SDHC, or SDXC cards) with a spring-loaded mechanism.

- **Insert the Memory Card**:
    - Gently insert your memory card into the slot with the metal connectors facing the camera's rear.

- o Push the card in until you hear a click, which indicates that the card is securely locked in place.
- **Close the Compartment**:
    - o Close the battery/memory card compartment door, making sure it is securely shut to prevent dust or moisture from entering.

3. Checking the Battery and Memory Card Status

- **Power On the Camera**:
    - o After inserting the battery and memory card, turn on the camera to check if the camera recognizes both the battery and the memory card.
- **Battery Level**:
    - o The camera will display the battery level on the screen or through the viewfinder. Ensure the battery is charged and ready for use.
- **Memory Card Status**:
    - o If the memory card is correctly inserted, the camera should recognize it and display the available space on the memory card. If there's an error, the camera will prompt you to check the card or reinsert it.

2.4 Powering On/Off the Camera

Turning your Nikon P950 on and off is simple. Here's a step-by-step guide to power the camera up or down:

Powering On the Camera

1. **Locate the Power Button**:
    - o The power button is located on the top right of the camera, near the shutter button.
2. **Turn the Camera On**:
    - o Press the **power button** to turn the camera on.
    - o The camera's LCD screen or electronic viewfinder (EVF) will light up, indicating that it is powered on. You may also hear the lens extending as it prepares for use.

Powering Off the Camera

1. **Locate the Power Button**:
    - o Again, find the **power button** near the shutter button on the top right of the camera.
2. **Turn the Camera Off**:
    - o Press and hold the **power button** for a brief moment until the camera turns off.
    - o The LCD screen and viewfinder will turn off, and the lens will retract back into the camera body.

Important Notes:

- **Automatic Power Off:**
    - The Nikon P950 has an automatic power-off function that will turn off the camera after a period of inactivity to save battery life. You can adjust this time in the camera's settings if needed.
- **Lens Retracting:**
    - After powering off, the lens will automatically retract into the camera body. Ensure that the lens cap is properly on to avoid dust or dirt getting into the lens.

2.5 Setting the Date, Time, and Language

When you first use your Nikon P950, it's important to set the correct date, time, and language to ensure that your photos and videos are properly labelled and that the camera interface is in your preferred language. Here's how to do it:

1. Turning On the Camera

- Press the **Power button** located on the top of the camera to turn it on.

2. Setting the Language

- **When You Turn the Camera On for the First Time:**
    - The camera will automatically prompt you to choose a language.
- **To Set or Change the Language Later:**
    - Press the **Menu button** located on the back of the camera.
    - In the menu, use the **Multi-Selector** (joystick) to navigate to the **Setup Menu** (wrench icon).
    - Select **Language** and press **OK**.
    - A list of available languages will appear on the screen. Scroll through the list and select your desired language.
    - Press **OK** to confirm your selection.

3. Setting the Date and Time

- **Initial Setup:**
    - After selecting your language, the camera will prompt you to set the date and time.
    - The **Date/Time** setting screen will appear with options to set the year, month, day, hour, and minute.
- **To Set or Change the Date and Time Later:**
    - Press the **Menu button** and navigate to the **Setup Menu** (wrench icon).

- Scroll down to the **Date/Time** setting and select it.
- Use the **Multi-Selector** to adjust the year, month, day, hour, and minute.
- Press the **Multi-Selector (OK)** button to confirm each setting. The camera will automatically save your settings.

- **Time Zone Setting**:
    - After setting the date and time, you may be prompted to select your time zone. Use the **Multi-Selector** to select the correct time zone based on your location.
    - Press **OK** to confirm your time zone.

4. **Confirming the Settings**

- Once you've set the date, time, and language, press **OK** to confirm your settings.
- The camera will return to the normal shooting mode, and your date, time, and language preferences will be applied.

CHAPTER THREE
BASIC OPERATIONS

3.1 Understanding the Mode Dial

The Mode Dial on the Nikon P950 is a critical component that allows you to quickly switch between different shooting modes to control how the camera captures images. Each mode offers specific settings that suit various photography styles and situations. Here's an overview of what each mode on the dial means:

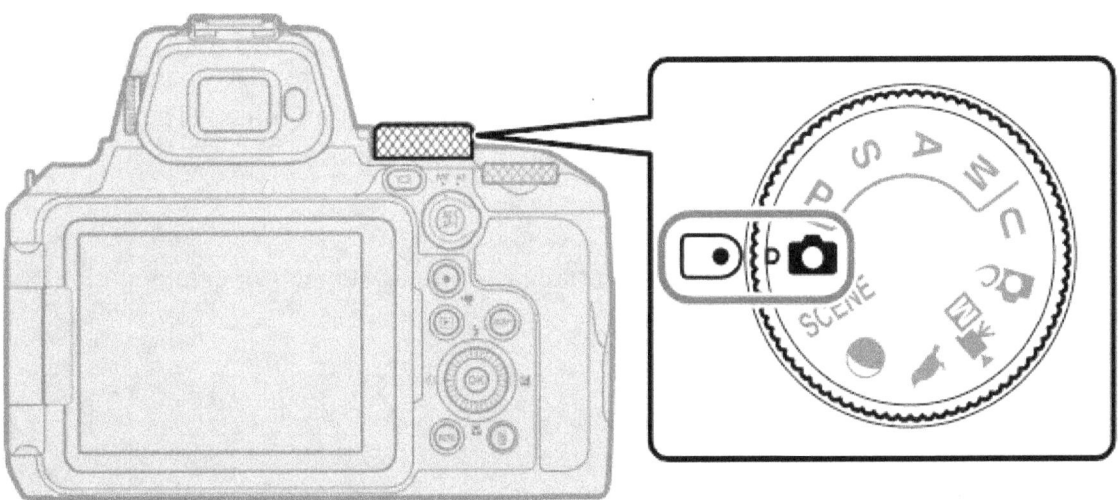

1. Auto Mode (Green Auto Icon)

- **Description**:
    - In this mode, the camera automatically adjusts all settings (such as aperture, shutter speed, and ISO) for you, making it the easiest mode for beginners or casual users.

- **When to Use**:
    - Use this mode when you want to capture photos with minimal effort and let the camera handle the technical aspects.

2. Program Mode (P)

- **Description**:
    - In Program mode, the camera automatically selects both the aperture and shutter speed, but you can adjust other settings like ISO, white balance, and flash.

- **When to Use**:
    - This mode is great for users who want more control over settings while still leaving some of the decision-making to the camera.

3. Aperture Priority Mode (A)

- **Description**:
  - In Aperture Priority (A) mode, you manually set the aperture (f-stop) to control the depth of field (how much of the image is in focus). The camera will automatically adjust the shutter speed to achieve a correct exposure.

- **When to Use**:
  - Use this mode if you want to control how much of the image is sharp or blurred, such as for portrait photography or shots with a shallow depth of field.

4. Shutter Priority Mode (S)

- **Description**:
  - In Shutter Priority (S) mode, you manually set the shutter speed to control how motion is captured (fast for freezing action, slow for motion blur). The camera will automatically adjust the aperture to maintain proper exposure.

- **When to Use**:
  - Use this mode when you want to capture fast-moving subjects or create motion blur in images.

5. Manual Mode (M)

- **Description**:
  - In Manual mode, you have full control over both aperture and shutter speed. You're responsible for achieving the correct exposure by adjusting both settings.

- **When to Use**:
  - Use Manual mode when you want complete creative control over your exposure settings. This is ideal for advanced users or when shooting in challenging lighting conditions.

6. Scene Modes (SCENE)

- **Description**:
  - The Scene Modes offer preset settings tailored to specific types of photography, such as portraits, landscapes, or night scenes. These are designed to optimize settings for common situations without needing to manually adjust everything.

- **When to Use**:
  - Use Scene modes when shooting in specific scenarios like low light, action, or close-ups. Popular options include:
    - **Portrait**: Optimized for taking portraits with a blurred background.
    - **Landscape**: Optimized for capturing wide vistas with a deep depth of field.
    - **Sports**: Optimized for fast-moving subjects.

- **Night Portrait**: Designed for portraits taken in low light, with flash and long exposure.
- **Macro**: Best for close-up photography of small subjects.

7. Effects Mode (EFFECTS)

- **Description**:
  - In Effects mode, you can add creative effects to your photos, such as black-and-white, sepia, or other artistic filters.
- **When to Use**:
  - Use this mode when you want to add a creative touch to your photos without editing them later.

8. Movie Mode (Movie Camera Icon)

- **Description**:
  - In Movie Mode, you can shoot high-definition video. The camera will adjust settings such as exposure and focus, but you can also manually control some features.
- **When to Use**:
  - Use this mode when you want to capture videos instead of photos.

9. Custom Modes (User Defined, U1/U2)

- **Description**:
  - The Nikon P950 allows you to save your favorite settings to custom modes (U1 and U2). These modes enable you to quickly access frequently used settings for specific shooting situations.
- **When to Use**:
  - Use custom modes when you have certain settings you frequently use for specific types of photos, like wildlife or low-light photography.

3.2 Using the Viewfinder and LCD Screen

The Nikon P950 offers both an electronic viewfinder (EVF) and a vari-angle LCD screen, providing flexibility depending on your shooting preferences and the environment. Here's a guide on how to use both:

1. Using the Electronic Viewfinder (EVF)

The **electronic viewfinder (EVF)** is ideal for more traditional photography. It gives you a digital view of your scene, and it's useful in bright conditions where the LCD screen may be hard to see.

How to Use the EVF:

1. **Activating the EVF**:
   - The EVF automatically activates when you bring the camera up to your eye.
   - If the EVF does not automatically turn on, press the **Viewfinder/LCD button** on the back of the camera to toggle between the EVF and the LCD screen.

2. **Adjusting the Viewfinder**:
   - The Nikon P950's EVF has a **diopter adjustment** on the side of the viewfinder. Use this dial to adjust the viewfinder for your eyesight, ensuring a clear image without needing glasses.

3. **Previewing Settings**:
   - The EVF shows real-time data, such as focus points, exposure information, and the settings you've selected (shutter speed, aperture, ISO). This allows you to preview how the camera's settings affect your image before you take the shot.

When to Use the EVF:

- **Bright sunlight**: The EVF provides better visibility in bright outdoor conditions where the LCD screen might be difficult to read.
- **More stability**: Holding the camera against your face helps steady the camera, which is especially useful when using telephoto zoom.

2. Using the Vari-Angle LCD Screen

The **vari-angle LCD screen** is a versatile display that can tilt and rotate to allow for comfortable shooting from a variety of angles, whether you're taking selfies, capturing high-angle shots, or getting low to the ground.

How to Use the LCD Screen:

1. **Activating the LCD Screen**:
   - The LCD screen automatically activates when you switch to the **LCD mode** by pressing the **Viewfinder/LCD button** on the back of the camera.

2. **Tilting and Rotating the Screen**:
   - Pull the LCD screen out from the back of the camera. It can rotate 180 degrees for self-shooting or 90 degrees for low or high-angle shots.
   - **Self-portrait or vlogging**: Rotate the screen to face forward so you can monitor your shot as you take it.
   - **High/low-angle shots**: Tilt the screen for easier composition when the camera is held above your head or near the ground.

3. **Touchscreen Functionality**:
    - The LCD screen is a **touchscreen**, allowing you to tap to set the focus point or adjust settings like exposure, ISO, and white balance.
    - You can also swipe and pinch to zoom in or out when reviewing photos.

When to Use the LCD Screen:

- **For flexible shooting angles**: The vari-angle feature is perfect for capturing shots at challenging angles, such as from above or below.
- **Video recording**: The LCD screen is especially useful for composing shots when recording video, especially when you need to see yourself or your framing in real-time.

3. Switching Between the EVF and LCD Screen

You can easily toggle between the **EVF** and the **LCD screen** by pressing the **Viewfinder/LCD button** on the back of the camera. The camera will automatically switch to the viewfinder when you bring it up to your eye, and back to the LCD screen when you move the camera away from your face. You can also press the button manually to switch between the two.

4. Adjusting Display Brightness

Both the EVF and LCD screen offer brightness adjustment for optimal visibility. This can be particularly useful in challenging lighting conditions, such as when you're shooting outdoors in bright sunlight or indoors in low light.

How to Adjust Brightness:

1. Press the **Menu** button and navigate to the **Display Brightness** setting in the camera's setup menu.
2. Adjust the brightness level to suit your environment.
3. Alternatively, some models also allow you to adjust brightness directly through the EVF or LCD screen's on-screen menu.

Both the **electronic viewfinder** and the **vari-angle LCD screen** offer distinct advantages depending on your shooting style and the situation. The EVF is perfect for stability and visibility in bright conditions, while the LCD screen provides flexibility and ease for composing shots at unconventional angles or during video recording.

3.3 Adjusting the Zoom (Optical and Digital)

The Nikon P950 is equipped with a powerful 83x optical zoom lens and offers digital zoom as well. Understanding how to adjust both zoom types will help you achieve the best results for various shooting situations. Here's a guide on using both optical and digital zoom effectively:

1. Optical Zoom

The **optical zoom** is the true zoom, achieved by physically adjusting the lens to magnify the subject without losing image quality. The P950's **83x optical zoom** gives you an impressive range, making it ideal for both wide-angle shots and extreme telephoto zooms.

Steps to Use Optical Zoom:

1. **Zoom In or Out**:
    - On the **lens barrel**, you'll find the **zoom ring** (or zoom control) which allows you to adjust the zoom manually.
    - To zoom in, rotate the **zoom ring** towards the **telephoto (T)** end (marked with a "T" or a **longer focal length**).
    - To zoom out, rotate the ring towards the **wide-angle (W)** end (marked with a "W" or **shorter focal length**).

2. **Zoom Control on the Camera**:
    - Alternatively, you can also use the **zoom lever** located near the shutter button. The zoom lever is a more convenient way to adjust zoom quickly:
        - Push the lever **forward** to zoom in.
        - Pull the lever **backward** to zoom out.
    - This allows for smooth, gradual zooming, whether you're capturing distant subjects or wide landscapes.

When to Use Optical Zoom:

- **For high-quality zooming**: Optical zoom preserves image quality, and you should always use it for subjects that require a higher level of detail, such as wildlife photography or sports.
- **For close-up shots**: Optical zoom allows you to get up close to distant subjects without sacrificing clarity.

2. Digital Zoom

Digital zoom is a method where the camera crops the center of the image and enlarges it, simulating a zoom effect. While convenient, it may result in a loss of image quality since you are essentially enlarging a portion of the image.

Steps to Use Digital Zoom:

1. **Activate Digital Zoom**:
   - Digital zoom is automatically activated when you reach the maximum limit of the optical zoom (83x), and you continue zooming beyond that.
   - Alternatively, you can enable or disable **digital zoom** via the camera's settings menu.

2. **Zoom Beyond Optical Zoom**:
   - Once you have reached the maximum optical zoom (83x), the camera will automatically engage **digital zoom** if you continue to zoom in.
   - The **digital zoom** will provide additional magnification, but keep in mind that image quality may degrade as you zoom further.

When to Use Digital Zoom:

- **For extreme magnification**: If you need to get even closer to a distant subject and image quality is not a priority (for example, for quick snapshots where detail is less important).
- **Avoid overusing**: Since digital zoom reduces image sharpness and introduces pixelation, it's best to use it sparingly and in situations where detail is less crucial.

3. Combining Optical and Digital Zoom

While optical zoom gives you the best image quality, you can combine both **optical and digital zoom** to achieve greater magnification. The Nikon P950 allows you to use its **digital zoom** after reaching the optical zoom limit, enabling you to zoom up to **166x**. However, it's important to note that the quality of the image will degrade as you move further into the digital zoom range.

Tips for Optimal Zooming:

- **Use a tripod**: When zooming in to higher levels (especially with digital zoom), the camera is more sensitive to movement, which can cause blur. A tripod or stable surface will help ensure sharp results.
- **Avoid digital zoom for detailed shots**: Stick to optical zoom for shots where you need the highest quality, such as landscapes, wildlife, or distant objects.

3.4 Capturing Photos

The Nikon P950 is designed to make photo capturing easy, whether you're shooting landscapes, wildlife, or portraits. Here's a step-by-step guide to help you capture stunning photos:

1. Preparing the Camera for Shooting

Before taking your first photo, ensure your camera is ready:

1. **Power On**: Turn on the camera by rotating the **Power switch**.
2. **Check the Lens**: Ensure the lens is clean and free from smudges. If needed, gently wipe it with a soft cloth.

3. **Set the Mode**: Choose your desired shooting mode using the **Mode dial**. The Nikon P950 offers various modes, such as:
    - **Auto mode**: For automatic settings.
    - **Program mode (P)**: For automatic settings with some manual adjustments.
    - **Aperture priority (A)**: Control the aperture while the camera automatically adjusts shutter speed.
    - **Shutter priority (S)**: Control the shutter speed while the camera adjusts the aperture.
    - **Manual (M)**: Full manual control over both aperture and shutter speed.
    - **Scene modes**: Specific settings for different scenes like portrait, landscape, or night portrait.

2. Adjusting the Zoom and Focus

1. **Zooming**:
    - Adjust the zoom to frame your subject. Use the **zoom lever** near the shutter button or the **zoom ring** on the lens to zoom in or out.
    - You can zoom up to **83x optical zoom** for distant subjects or use **digital zoom** for even greater magnification, though quality may degrade.

2. **Focusing**:
    - **Auto-focus (AF)**: The camera will focus on the subject automatically. Half-press the **shutter button** to activate autofocus. The camera will lock focus when it's ready, indicated by a green focus confirmation on the screen.
    - **Manual focus**: If you need more control over focus, you can manually adjust it via the camera's settings.

3. Composing the Shot

1. **Using the Viewfinder or LCD**:
    - **Viewfinder**: If you prefer a more traditional shooting experience, use the **electronic viewfinder (EVF)**. Bring the camera to your eye, and the EVF will automatically turn on.
    - **LCD screen**: Use the **vari-angle LCD screen** if you need to shoot from difficult angles (e.g., overhead shots, low-angle shots, or selfies).

2. **Setting the Exposure**:
    - **Exposure Compensation**: Adjust the exposure if your image is too bright or too dark. You can find the **Exposure Compensation dial** on the camera to increase or decrease exposure by ±3 stops.
    - **ISO**: The ISO setting controls the camera's sensitivity to light. In low-light situations, increase the ISO (e.g., 800 or 1600) to ensure proper exposure, but be cautious as higher ISO settings may introduce noise.

- **Shutter Speed**: A faster shutter speed (e.g., 1/1000s) freezes motion, while a slower shutter speed (e.g., 1/30s) is useful for capturing movement or long exposures.

3. **White Balance**:
    - Adjust the **White Balance** to match the lighting conditions. The P950 has presets for different lighting situations like sunlight, cloudy, fluorescent, and more.

4. Capturing the Photo

Once your settings are adjusted and your composition is ready, take the shot:

1. **Half-Press the Shutter Button**: This activates the camera's **autofocus** and **exposure metering**.
2. **Press the Shutter Button Fully**: Once the camera confirms focus and exposure, press the shutter fully to capture the image.

5. Reviewing Your Photos

1. **Playback Mode**: After capturing a photo, press the **Playback button** on the back of the camera to review your shots.
2. **Zooming In**: In playback mode, use the **zoom lever** to zoom into your photo and check for focus and details.
3. **Delete or Retake**: If you're not happy with the shot, you can delete it and try again by pressing the **Delete button**.

6. Tips for Better Photos

- **Use a Tripod**: For stable shots, especially in low light or when zooming in on distant subjects.
- **Lighting**: Pay attention to the lighting conditions. Soft, even lighting (e.g., during the golden hour) can make a significant difference in the quality of your photos.
- **Rule of Thirds**: Use the rule of thirds to frame your subject. The P950 offers grid lines in the viewfinder and LCD to help with this composition.
- **Depth of Field**: Adjust the aperture (in aperture priority mode) to control the depth of field. A wider aperture (e.g., f/2.8) will blur the background, while a smaller aperture (e.g., f/8) will keep more of the scene in focus.

7. Special Photo Features

The Nikon P950 also includes various features to enhance your photography:

1. **Time-lapse Mode**: Perfect for capturing the movement of clouds or the transition from day to night.
2. **Continuous Shooting**: Useful for action shots or capturing a series of moments. Hold the shutter button down, and the camera will take multiple shots in quick succession.
3. **Scene Modes**: Choose preset modes for specific scenarios like portraits, landscapes, or night shots, which adjust settings automatically for optimal results.

3.5 Recording Videos

The Nikon P950 is not only an excellent still photography camera but also a powerful tool for recording high-quality videos. With its **4K UHD video capabilities**, powerful zoom, and user-friendly features, you can capture stunning footage in a variety of settings. Here's how to make the most of your video recording experience with the Nikon P950:

1. Preparing the Camera for Video Recording

Before you begin recording, make sure your camera is ready:

1. **Power On**: Turn on the camera by rotating the **Power switch**.
2. **Set the Mode**: Switch the **Mode dial** to the **video recording mode**:
   - Select **Auto** for automatic video recording settings, or switch to **Manual (M)**, **Aperture Priority (A)**, or **Shutter Priority (S)** if you want more control over your settings.
   - You can also use **Scene modes** (such as "Night" or "Sports") for specific recording conditions.
3. **Adjust Settings**:
   - **Resolution**: Choose your preferred resolution. The Nikon P950 supports **4K UHD (3840 x 2160)** at 30p and **Full HD (1920 x 1080)** at 60p.
   - **Frame Rate**: For smooth motion, select 60p (60 frames per second) for fast-moving subjects. For cinematic looks, choose 24p or 30p.
   - **Audio Settings**: Make sure to check the **microphone input** and adjust the **audio levels** if necessary, especially for external microphones.
   - **Focus Mode**: You can select **Continuous Autofocus (AF-C)** for smooth focus transitions during recording.

2. Starting the Video Recording

Once the camera is prepared, you're ready to start recording:

1. **Enter Video Mode**:
   - Press the **Red Movie Record button** on the back of the camera to start recording.
   - The **LCD screen** or **EVF** will show a red recording icon, indicating that the camera is actively recording.
2. **Zoom During Recording**:
   - Use the **zoom lever** or **zoom ring** to zoom in or out while recording. The P950's **83x optical zoom** lets you smoothly transition between wide-angle and telephoto shots during video.
   - **Note**: The **digital zoom** can also be used in video mode, but it may reduce the image quality.

3. **Focus While Recording**:
    - If using **autofocus**, the camera will adjust focus during recording to keep your subject sharp.
    - **Manual focus**: You can adjust focus manually using the **focus ring** or the **focus slider** on the touchscreen for more precise control during video recording.

4. **Recording Time Limit**:
    - The Nikon P950 records videos without a strict time limit, but be aware that the camera may stop recording if it overheats or exceeds memory card space. Ensure you have a **large-capacity memory card** (e.g., 64GB or higher) for longer recordings.

3. While Recording: Additional Controls and Features

The Nikon P950 offers several features that enhance your video recording experience:

1. **Exposure Control**:
    - If you want to adjust exposure manually during recording, switch to **manual exposure** mode and control the **shutter speed** and **aperture**.
    - **Exposure Compensation**: Adjust exposure compensation to brighten or darken the scene.

2. **White Balance**:
    - Manually adjust the **white balance** to suit different lighting conditions for more accurate colour reproduction.

3. **Stabilization**:
    - The P950 features **Hybrid VR (Vibration Reduction)** for stabilizing handheld video recordings, minimizing shakiness.
    - **Use a tripod** for even more stability, especially in low-light or zoomed-in shooting situations.

4. Stopping and Reviewing the Video

1. **Stop Recording**:
    - Press the **Red Movie Record button** again to stop recording. The camera will save the video file to the memory card.

2. **Playback Your Video**:
    - Press the **Playback button** to review your video.
    - Use the **zoom lever** to zoom in and check for focus and details, or swipe the touchscreen to scroll through the footage.

5. Tips for Better Video Recording

1. **Use a Tripod or Stabilizer**: For smoother video, especially with telephoto zoom or handheld shots.

2. **Lighting**: Make sure your subject is well-lit. Consider using natural light or external lighting for better results, particularly in low-light conditions.

3. **Audio**: Use an **external microphone** for better audio quality. The camera's built-in microphone may pick up unwanted noise.

4. **Focus Transitions**: For professional-looking video, use smooth and gradual focus transitions, either through **manual focus** or the camera's **autofocus system**.

5. **Time-Lapse Video**: The Nikon P950 also supports time-lapse recording, which can be used to capture long-term processes, like sunsets or city traffic.

6. Using Advanced Video Features

1. **Slow Motion**:
   - The P950 allows you to shoot in **slow-motion** by adjusting the frame rate to higher values (e.g., 120p in 1080p). This is ideal for capturing fast-moving subjects with dramatic effects.

2. **Time-Lapse**:
   - Use the **Time-Lapse feature** to create stunning videos of long events, such as clouds moving or flowers blooming.

CHAPTER FOUR
SHOOTING MODES

4.1 Auto Mode

The Auto Mode on the Nikon P950 is designed for users who want to capture high-quality photos and videos without worrying about adjusting settings manually. It's perfect for beginners or anyone who needs to quickly capture a moment without adjusting the camera's settings.

1. What Auto Mode Does

In **Auto Mode**, the camera automatically adjusts the essential settings, including:

- **Shutter Speed**: The camera selects the appropriate shutter speed based on the scene to avoid motion blur.
- **Aperture**: The camera adjusts the aperture (f-stop) for the optimal depth of field, keeping your subject in focus.
- **ISO**: The camera automatically sets the ISO based on the available light, ensuring a properly exposed image.
- **White Balance**: The camera detects the lighting conditions and adjusts the white balance for natural-looking colours.
- **Focus**: The camera automatically focuses on the main subject, making sure your photos are sharp.

This mode is ideal for users who want to take the guesswork out of their photography and let the camera do the heavy lifting.

2. Using Auto Mode

1. **Set the Mode Dial to Auto**:
   - Turn the **Mode dial** on the top of the camera to the **green Auto mode (Auto)**. This will activate automatic settings for both still photos and video.

2. **Frame Your Shot**:
   - Use the **LCD screen** or **electronic viewfinder (EVF)** to compose your image. The camera will automatically adjust settings for exposure, focus, and other parameters to match the scene.

3. **Capture the Photo**:
   - Half-press the **shutter button** to activate autofocus. The camera will focus on the subject and display a focus indicator.
   - Once focus is confirmed, press the **shutter button fully** to capture the image.

4. **Recording Video in Auto Mode**:
    - In Auto mode, you can also record video by pressing the **Red Movie Record button**. The camera will automatically adjust the settings, including exposure, focus, and zoom, for video recording.

3. Benefits of Auto Mode

- **Ease of Use**: Perfect for beginners or those who don't want to worry about manual settings. The camera handles everything automatically.

- **Quick Capture**: Auto Mode is great for spontaneous moments when you need to capture a photo or video without wasting time adjusting settings.

- **Reliable Exposure**: The camera does a good job of adjusting exposure, even in challenging lighting conditions (e.g., bright sunlight or low-light environments).

- **Sharp Focus**: The camera will select the correct focus point, ensuring your main subject is sharp.

4. Limitations of Auto Mode

While **Auto Mode** is excellent for quick and easy shooting, there are some limitations:

- **Limited Creative Control**: The camera makes all the decisions, so you don't have control over settings like aperture or shutter speed, which can limit your creativity.

- **May Not Always Be Optimal**: In certain situations, such as low light or fast-moving subjects, the camera might not always choose the best settings. You may want to switch to other modes (like **Aperture Priority** or **Shutter Priority**) for more control over exposure or motion.

- **Zoom Control**: While the camera adjusts focus and exposure, you still control zoom. In Auto Mode, the zoom operates in a more "automatic" fashion, but manual zoom adjustments can provide better results in some situations.

5. When to Use Auto Mode

- **Everyday Use**: Auto Mode is great for casual photography when you don't want to spend time adjusting settings, such as capturing family moments, vacations, or outdoor activities.

- **Quick Shots**: When you're on the go or need to capture fast-moving subjects, Auto Mode ensures you can get the shot without any delay.

- **Beginner Photographers**: For users who are just starting with photography, Auto Mode simplifies the process by handling all the settings for you.

6. Moving Beyond Auto Mode

Once you become more comfortable with the camera, you might want to explore other modes to gain more control over your photos:

- **Program Mode (P)**: Offers more flexibility while keeping most of the settings automatic.

- **Aperture Priority (A)**: Control the depth of field by adjusting the aperture while the camera automatically sets the shutter speed.

- **Shutter Priority (S)**: Control motion by adjusting the shutter speed while the camera manages the aperture.
- **Manual Mode (M)**: Take full control of both aperture and shutter speed for complete creative freedom.

The **Auto Mode** on the Nikon P950 is a fantastic starting point for capturing great photos and videos without needing to worry about camera settings. It simplifies the process while still delivering excellent results for a wide range of subjects and situations.

4.2 Scene Modes

Scene Modes on the Nikon P950 are preset configurations that automatically adjust the camera's settings to suit specific shooting conditions or subjects. These modes allow you to optimize your photos without needing to manually tweak settings like aperture, shutter speed, ISO, or white balance. Scene Modes are perfect for capturing high-quality images in different environments, making it easier for both beginners and experienced users to get the best results.

1. Accessing Scene Modes

To use Scene Modes on the Nikon P950:

1. Turn the **Mode dial** on the top of the camera to **SCENE**.
2. Once in Scene Mode, you can scroll through various scene presets using the camera's **Menu** or the **multiselector** buttons on the back.
3. Select the appropriate scene for your shooting situation.

2. Scene Modes Available on the Nikon P950

Here are the common **Scene Modes** and the types of situations for which they are best suited:

- **Portrait**:
  - Ideal for capturing portraits of people.
  - The camera adjusts the settings for a shallow depth of field, ensuring that the subject is sharp while the background is softly blurred.
  - **Best for**: Close-up shots of people or animals, focusing on facial details.
- **Landscape**:
  - Designed for wide-angle shots of landscapes, ensuring that both the foreground and background are in focus.
  - The camera selects a small aperture (high f-stop) for a large depth of field, ensuring everything is sharp.
  - **Best for**: Outdoor landscapes, cityscapes, and scenic views.

- **Night Portrait**:
  - This mode is optimized for low-light settings, where you want to capture both the subject and the background at night.
  - The camera uses a slower shutter speed to allow more light into the sensor and fires the flash to illuminate the subject.
  - **Best for**: Portraits in low-light or night settings, such as evening events or nighttime city shots.
- **Sports**:
  - Designed for fast-moving subjects, this mode prioritizes a fast shutter speed to freeze motion.
  - The camera will also adjust the ISO for faster shutter speeds to capture sharp, clear action shots.
  - **Best for**: Sports, animals, or any action shots where the subject is moving quickly.
- **Close-Up (Macro)**:
  - This mode is optimized for photographing small subjects at close range, such as flowers or insects.
  - The camera ensures that the subject is sharp while allowing for a blurred background.
  - **Best for**: Macro photography, such as shots of flowers, insects, or small objects.
- **Night Scene**:
  - Best for capturing city lights, starry skies, or any low-light scene without a subject.
  - The camera uses a slow shutter speed to capture as much light as possible and produces sharp, well-lit nighttime photos.
  - **Best for**: Night landscapes, city lights, and scenes with ambient lighting.
- **Sunset**:
  - This mode is designed for capturing sunsets with rich, warm colors.
  - The camera adjusts settings to enhance reds, oranges, and yellows for more vibrant sunset photos.
  - **Best for**: Sunset shots, capturing the beauty of the golden hour.
- **Dawn/Dusk**:
  - Ideal for early morning or late evening shots when the lighting is soft and muted.
  - This mode adjusts the exposure to preserve the subtle colors of the scene.
  - **Best for**: Early morning or late evening outdoor photos with soft lighting.

- **Beach/Snow**:
    - This mode is designed for shooting in bright environments, like beaches or snow-covered landscapes.
    - It compensates for the bright reflections off the sand or snow, ensuring that the exposure is balanced and the scene is not overexposed.
    - **Best for**: Beach scenes, snow photography, or any bright, reflective surfaces.
- **Fireworks**:
    - Perfect for capturing fireworks displays with long exposures to capture trails of light and vibrant colours.
    - The camera uses a slow shutter speed to capture the full effect of the fireworks' motion.
    - **Best for**: Fireworks displays or any event with bright lights in motion.
- **Party/Indoor**:
    - Designed for indoor events or low-light scenes, this mode uses a slower shutter speed and boosts ISO to brighten up dark indoor environments.
    - The camera also adjusts the flash to balance lighting and create natural-looking photos.
    - **Best for**: Indoor parties, events, or any low-light indoor photography.
- **Autumn Colours**:
    - Optimized for capturing vibrant fall colours, such as reds, oranges, and yellows, with enhanced saturation.
    - This mode enhances the warm colours of autumn for more dramatic and lively images.
    - **Best for**: Autumn scenes, forests, or any environment with rich foliage.
- **Food**:
    - This mode adjusts for the best colour and sharpness when photographing food. It ensures that colours appear vibrant and natural.
    - **Best for**: Food photography, capturing the textures and colours of dishes.
- **Pet Portrait**:
    - Specifically designed for taking portraits of pets, this mode ensures that the camera focuses on the pet's face while minimizing distractions in the background.
    - **Best for**: Pet photography, capturing animals with clear detail.

3. Tips for Using Scene Modes

- **Lighting Conditions**: Scene Modes are designed to optimize settings based on typical lighting conditions for that particular scene. Pay attention to lighting, as it can still affect the outcome of your photo.

- **Camera Movement**: Some Scene Modes, like **Night Scene** and **Fireworks**, require steady hands or a tripod for longer exposures. Use a tripod whenever possible for sharper images.
- **Flash Control**: In modes like **Night Portrait** or **Indoor**, the camera may automatically use the flash. If you prefer to avoid using the flash, you can turn it off manually.

4. When to Use Scene Modes

- **Convenience**: When you need to quickly set up your camera for specific scenes or subjects without worrying about technical settings.
- **Beginners**: If you're just starting with photography and don't want to dive into manual settings, Scene Modes will help you get the best results with minimal effort.
- **Special Occasions**: Scene Modes are excellent for capturing specific moments, such as fireworks displays, night-time portraits, or autumn colors, with the best settings for those environments.

Scene Modes on the Nikon P950 make it easy to capture stunning photos in a variety of situations without the need for manual adjustments. Whether you're taking portraits, landscapes, or shooting a fast-moving subject, Scene Modes ensure you're always prepared to capture the perfect shot.

4.3 Manual Modes (P, S, A, M)

The manual modes (P, S, A, and M) on the Nikon P950 offer more control over your camera settings, allowing you to create more personalized and creative images compared to Auto or Scene Modes. These modes give you the flexibility to control various aspects of your exposure, like shutter speed, aperture, ISO, and focus, depending on the mode you choose. Understanding each mode will help you get the most out of your Nikon P950 for different shooting scenarios.

1. Program Mode (P)

Program Mode (P) is a semi-automatic mode that offers flexibility while still automating some aspects of exposure. The camera automatically adjusts both **shutter speed** and **aperture** to ensure a properly exposed image, but you can still control other settings, such as **ISO**.

- **What it does**: The camera selects the shutter speed and aperture combination for a correct exposure, while you can adjust other settings, such as ISO or white balance.
- **How to use it**:
    1. Turn the **Mode dial** to **P** (Program).
    2. The camera automatically selects the optimal settings for shutter speed and aperture.
    3. You can adjust the **ISO** and other settings if needed, and the camera will recalculate exposure accordingly.
    4. You can also shift the program by rotating the **command dial**, which changes the aperture and shutter speed combination while keeping the exposure balanced.
- **Best for**: Users who want to shoot quickly but still want to control some of the settings, such as ISO or white balance, without worrying about aperture and shutter speed.

2. Shutter Priority Mode (S)

In **Shutter Priority Mode** (S), you control the **shutter speed**, while the camera automatically adjusts the **aperture** to maintain the correct exposure.

- **What it does**: You set the shutter speed to capture motion as desired, and the camera automatically adjusts the aperture to ensure proper exposure.
- **How to use it**:
    1. Turn the **Mode dial** to **S** (Shutter Priority).
    2. Use the **command dial** to set your desired **shutter speed**. Faster shutter speeds (e.g., 1/1000) freeze motion, while slower speeds (e.g., 1/30) create motion blur.
    3. The camera will automatically adjust the aperture to balance exposure.
    4. You can also adjust **ISO** and **white balance** as needed.
- **Best for**: Capturing fast-moving subjects (e.g., sports, wildlife) where you want to control motion blur, or creating intentional motion blur (e.g., flowing water or light trails).

3. Aperture Priority Mode (A)

Aperture Priority Mode (A) gives you control over the **aperture**, while the camera automatically adjusts the **shutter speed** to maintain a balanced exposure.

- **What it does**: You set the **aperture** to control the depth of field (the amount of the scene in focus), and the camera automatically adjusts the shutter speed.
- **How to use it**:
    1. Turn the **Mode dial** to **A** (Aperture Priority).
    2. Use the **command dial** to set the desired **aperture (f-stop)**. A larger aperture (e.g., f/2.8) creates a shallow depth of field (blurry background), while a smaller aperture (e.g., f/11) provides more depth of field (sharp foreground and background).
    3. The camera will automatically adjust the **shutter speed** to achieve the correct exposure.
    4. You can adjust **ISO** and **white balance** if needed.
- **Best for**: Portraits, where you want to control the background blur (bokeh), or landscapes, where you want everything in focus.

4. Manual Mode (M)

Manual Mode (M) gives you full control over both **shutter speed** and **aperture**. You are responsible for setting both parameters, as well as **ISO**, to ensure the correct exposure.

- **What it does**: You manually set both the **shutter speed** and **aperture**. You can also control **ISO** and fine-tune other settings such as white balance and exposure compensation.
- **How to use it**:
    1. Turn the **Mode dial** to **M** (Manual).

2. Set the **shutter speed** using the **command dial**.

3. Set the **aperture** using the **other dial** or the **command dial**.

4. Adjust the **ISO** to suit the lighting conditions. If needed, use the **exposure indicator** on the screen to help you fine-tune your settings for proper exposure.

5. You may also use a **light meter** (in the camera's viewfinder or LCD) to assist in adjusting both settings for correct exposure.

- **Best for**: Experienced photographers who want complete control over exposure settings, allowing for full creative control and precise adjustments for specific lighting conditions.

5. When to Use Each Mode

- **Program Mode (P)**: When you want to quickly capture images with automatic settings, but still want the flexibility to adjust **ISO** and other parameters.

- **Shutter Priority (S)**: When you want to freeze fast-moving subjects or intentionally blur motion while leaving the camera to select the right aperture.

- **Aperture Priority (A)**: When you want to control the depth of field for selective focus, such as blurring the background in portraits or ensuring everything is sharp in landscapes.

- **Manual Mode (M)**: When you need complete control over both shutter speed and aperture for creative and professional work, especially in tricky lighting conditions or for advanced techniques like long exposure photography.

6. Additional Tips for Manual Modes

- **'Exposure Triangle**: Understanding the relationship between **shutter speed**, **aperture**, and **ISO** is essential when using manual modes. Adjust one setting while monitoring the others to achieve the desired exposure.

    - **Shutter Speed**: Controls motion blur and how long light hits the sensor.
    - **Aperture**: Controls the depth of field and the amount of light reaching the sensor.
    - **ISO**: Controls the sensitivity of the sensor to light, affecting exposure and noise levels.

- **Use a Tripod**: In **Manual Mode**, especially for long exposures, using a tripod can help prevent camera shake and ensure sharp images.

- **Exposure Compensation**: In Manual Mode, the camera won't automatically adjust for overexposure or underexposure, so use the **exposure indicator** to help you find the right balance.

- **Metering Mode**: Use different **metering modes** (e.g., **Matrix**, **Spot**, or **Center-weighted**) to control how the camera measures light in your scene.

The manual modes on the Nikon P950 (P, S, A, and M) provide a balance of control and automation, making them suitable for various photography scenarios, from quick snapshots to professional-level work. Whether you're capturing action, focusing on depth of field, or creating unique exposure effects, these modes offer the tools needed to bring your creative vision to life.

4.4 Birdwatching and Moon Mode

The Nikon P950 offers specialized modes for capturing subjects that require unique settings: Birdwatching Mode and Moon Mode. These modes are designed to optimize your camera's settings for photographing distant subjects, making them ideal for nature enthusiasts, especially those interested in wildlife photography and celestial photography.

1. Birdwatching Mode

Birdwatching Mode is a specialized mode on the Nikon P950, optimized for capturing birds and other fast-moving wildlife. This mode is perfect for those who enjoy photographing birds in flight or perched in trees, where focus speed, exposure, and zoom adjustments need to be quick and precise.

- **What it does**:
    - The camera automatically adjusts settings to help you capture sharp, well-exposed images of birds. It prioritizes fast shutter speeds, a wide aperture (for good light capture), and a high ISO (to deal with lighting variations).
    - The **autofocus system** is optimized for tracking moving subjects, ensuring that the camera quickly locks focus on the bird even when it's moving.

- **How to use it**:

1. Turn the **Mode dial** to **Birdwatching Mode** (this is typically found within the **Scene Modes**).
2. The camera will automatically adjust settings for optimal bird photography, including faster shutter speeds and higher ISO.
3. Use the **zoom control** to frame the bird, whether it's perched nearby or flying at a distance.
4. The camera uses **Continuous Autofocus** (AF-C) to track the subject and help keep the bird in focus as it moves.
5. If needed, you can adjust settings like **ISO** or **white balance** manually to fine-tune exposure, but the camera will generally provide the ideal automatic settings.

- **Best for**:
    - Capturing birds in flight or those moving quickly across the scene.
    - Birdwatching trips where subjects are often unpredictable and require quick camera responses.
    - Wildlife photography when the subject is far off and a fast, efficient autofocus is necessary.

2. Moon Mode

Moon Mode is another specialized setting on the Nikon P950, designed to help you capture the moon with exceptional detail, even in challenging lighting conditions. Since the moon is a bright object in a dark sky, this mode helps ensure proper exposure, sharpness, and contrast when photographing the moon.

- **What it does**:
    - The camera automatically adjusts the settings to properly expose the moon without overexposing the rest of the night sky.

- It uses a **smaller aperture** to maintain sharpness in the moon's details and adjusts the shutter speed to ensure the moon appears bright and well-defined without blowing out highlights.
- The mode also helps reduce noise in the dark areas of the photo, resulting in a clean image of the moon.

- **How to use it**:

1. Turn the **Mode dial** to **Moon Mode** (usually found under **Scene Modes**).
2. The camera will set the aperture, shutter speed, and ISO for optimal moon photography.
3. Use the **zoom** to frame the moon, adjusting for the best composition (e.g., a close-up or wide shot with surrounding stars).
4. The camera may also use a **tripod mode** setting to help prevent any motion blur, especially when using slower shutter speeds.
5. The camera will automatically balance the exposure to avoid overexposing the moon and preserve the details of its surface.

- **Best for**:
  - Capturing the moon in all its detail, especially during full moons or other special lunar events.
  - Night sky photography when you want to clearly capture the moon without losing surrounding detail, like stars.
  - Celestial photography, including lunar eclipses or super moons, where precise exposure is crucial.

3. Tips for Using Birdwatching and Moon Modes

- **Birdwatching Mode**:
  - **Continuous Focus**: Ensure the camera's **AF-C** (Continuous Autofocus) is engaged for tracking birds in flight. This mode will continuously focus on the moving subject.
  - **Shutter Speed**: Birdwatching requires fast shutter speeds to freeze motion. The camera in Birdwatching Mode will automatically adjust this, but you can adjust ISO or use a faster shutter speed if required.
  - **Stabilization**: For bird photography, especially when using the zoom lens to capture distant subjects, activate **Vibration Reduction (VR)** for steadier shots.

- **Moon Mode**:
  - **Tripod**: For the best results in **Moon Mode**, especially if you're using slow shutter speeds, a **tripod** is essential to avoid any camera shake or motion blur.
  - **Use a Remote Shutter Release**: Consider using a remote shutter release or the camera's self-timer to minimize any shake when pressing the shutter button.
  - **Manual Adjustments**: While **Moon Mode** is designed to handle most of the exposure adjustments, you can still fine-tune the image by manually adjusting **ISO** or **white balance** if needed.

Both Birdwatching Mode and Moon Mode are excellent examples of how the Nikon P950 simplifies shooting for specialized subjects. These modes adjust essential settings to ensure you get the best results with minimal effort, allowing you to focus on your composition rather than technicalities. Whether you're capturing the beauty of a bird in flight or photographing the moon on a clear night, these modes ensure that your shots will be as impressive as the subjects you're capturing.

4.5 Creative Effects

The Nikon P950 offers a range of creative effects that can add artistic flair to your photos and videos. These effects let you experiment with different visual styles, from vivid colour enhancements to artistic filters. The creative effects are accessible through the camera's scene modes, menu settings, and sometimes specific button presses, allowing you to easily customize your images and videos in ways that go beyond basic settings.

Here's an overview of some of the creative effects available on the Nikon P950:

1. Filter Effects

The Nikon P950 provides various filter effects that you can apply to your photos, instantly transforming their look. These filters are perfect for adding a unique touch to your images, especially in creative or artistic photography.

- **What it does**: The camera applies various colour adjustments, contrasts, and textures to your photos or videos, creating a distinctive look.

- **Types of filter effects**:
    - **Vivid**: Enhances colours, making them brighter and more saturated, perfect for capturing landscapes or flowers.
    - **Soft**: Adds a softening effect, blurring the image slightly for a dreamy or romantic feel.
    - **High Key**: Increases brightness, lightening the image, often used for portraits or fashion shots.
    - **Low Key**: Reduces brightness and contrast to create moody, darker images, suitable for dramatic portraits or artistic photography.
    - **Pop**: Increases saturation and contrast, giving the image a high-energy, bold appearance.
    - **Monochrome**: Converts the image to black and white, with different tonality effects like **sepia** or **high contrast**.

- **How to use it**:
1. Turn the **Mode dial** to **Creative Effects** or access them through the camera's **menu**.
2. Choose a filter effect from the available options.
3. Take your shot as usual, with the effect applied.

- **Best for**: Portraits, landscapes, nature shots, or whenever you want to give your photos a distinctive artistic touch.

2. Special Effects (Scene Modes)

The **Scene Modes** also include specialized effects that adjust the camera settings for specific creative outcomes. These modes automatically adjust your camera's exposure, focus, and other settings, while also applying artistic effects.

- **What it does**: Applies artistic effects to the scene you're shooting, perfect for specific creative situations.
- **Available Scene Modes with Special Effects**:
    - **Night Portrait**: Optimizes settings for shooting portraits at night, while creating a beautiful soft background blur.
    - **Sunset**: Enhances the warm tones of the sky and emphasizes the vivid colours of a sunset.
    - **Fireworks**: Designed for capturing long-exposure shots of fireworks, emphasizing the light trails and burst colours.
    - **Beach/Snow**: Increases brightness to compensate for the brightness of reflective surfaces like sand or snow, preventing underexposure.
    - **Party/Indoor**: Boosts colours and brightness in low light for more vibrant indoor shots.
- **How to use it**:

1. Turn the **Mode dial** to the **Scene Mode** (such as Night Portrait, Fireworks, etc.).
2. Select the relevant scene that matches your shooting situation.
3. The camera will automatically apply settings and creative effects for the chosen scene.

- **Best for**: Capturing specific scenes like sunsets, fireworks, or indoor parties with artistic and vibrant results.

3. Time-Lapse and Long Exposure Effects

The Nikon P950 also allows you to create unique time-lapse and long exposure shots, which are excellent for capturing motion in an artistic way or showing the passage of time.

- **What it does**:
    - **Time-Lapse**: The camera automatically takes a series of photos at set intervals, which can later be combined into a video that shows the gradual change over time.
    - **Long Exposure**: This effect involves keeping the shutter open for a longer period, allowing for the capture of motion blur (e.g., flowing water, moving clouds) or light trails (e.g., car lights at night).
- **How to use it**:

1. Go to the Scene Mode or Manual Mode to enable Time-Lapse or set the camera for Long Exposure.
2. For Time-Lapse, choose a time interval (e.g., every 5 seconds) and let the camera capture the scene over a longer period.

3. For Long Exposure, select a slower shutter speed and use a tripod to ensure sharp results, capturing the movement or light trails.
- **Best for**: Capturing moving subjects like clouds, water, or car lights (long exposure) or showcasing a time-progressing scene like a sunset or a bustling city street (time-lapse).

4. Creative Colour Options

The Nikon P950 offers **colour filters** and effects that can change the overall tone of your images or enhance specific elements. These include options for converting images to black and white or adding vibrant colour filters.

- **What it does**: Adjusts the image's colour balance, saturation, or tone to create a unique look.
- **Available Colour Effects**:
  - **Vivid Colour**: Makes the colours in your image more intense and saturated.
  - **Sepia**: Adds a warm, brownish tone to your images, giving them an old-time, vintage feel.
  - **High Contrast Black and White**: Produces strong contrasts between light and dark areas, ideal for creating dramatic monochrome photos.
- **How to use it**:

1. Select the **Creative Colour Effect** from the camera's **menu** or via the **Scene Modes**.
2. Choose the desired effect, such as **sepia** or **black and white**.
3. Take your photo with the applied effect.
- **Best for**: When you want to create unique, timeless images with a dramatic feel or when you want to emphasize certain parts of the photo by adjusting the colour tones.

5. Adding Creative Effects to Videos

In addition to photos, the Nikon P950 also allows you to apply creative effects to your video recordings, giving your clips a unique and stylized look.

- **What it does**: Allows you to apply filters and effects in real-time while shooting videos, such as:
  - **Slow Motion**: Captures fast-moving subjects in slow motion, enhancing the drama and impact.
  - **Time-Lapse**: Creates a sped-up video effect, ideal for showing long-term processes like a sunset or the movement of crowds.
  - **Filters**: Some of the same creative filters available for photos can also be applied to videos.
- **How to use it**:

1. Select the **Creative Video Mode** from the **Menu** or **Scene Modes**.
2. Choose a filter or effect (e.g., slow-motion, time-lapse).

3. Start recording your video with the effect applied in real-time.

- **Best for**: Videos where you want to create a more cinematic or creative look, such as adding slow-motion effects to a running scene or showcasing a dynamic time-lapse.

Tips for Using Creative Effects

- **Experiment with Different Effects**: Try combining different creative effects (e.g., using **vivid color** with **high key** brightness) to create bold, eye-catching images.

- **Use Tripods**: For effects like **long exposure** and **time-lapse**, using a tripod ensures stable images and videos, especially when shooting at slower shutter speeds or over long periods.

- **Preview Effects**: Before taking your shot, always preview the effect to ensure it aligns with your creative vision, adjusting settings if needed.

The Creative Effects on the Nikon P950 are a fun and powerful way to add artistic style to your photos and videos. Whether you're enhancing the colours in a landscape, applying a vintage filter to a portrait, or capturing the beauty of a night scene with long exposure, these effects can elevate your work and offer a more creative, personalized touch.

CHAPTER FIVE
ADVANCED PHOTOGRAPHY SETTINGS

5.1 Adjusting Exposure (ISO, Shutter Speed, Aperture)

The Nikon P950 allows users to control exposure by adjusting the three key settings that determine how light interacts with the camera sensor: ISO, shutter speed, and aperture. Understanding and mastering these settings will enable you to capture perfectly exposed photos in any lighting condition.

1. **Understanding Exposure Settings**

    1. **ISO**: Determines the camera sensor's sensitivity to light.
        - **Low ISO (e.g., 100)**: Best for bright conditions; produces minimal noise.
        - **High ISO (e.g., 1600 or higher)**: Ideal for low-light conditions but may introduce noise (graininess).
    2. **Shutter Speed**: Controls how long the shutter stays open.
        - **Fast Shutter Speed (e.g., 1/1000s)**: Freezes motion, perfect for action shots.
        - **Slow Shutter Speed (e.g., 1/10s)**: Captures motion blur or allows more light for night shots.
    3. **Aperture (f-stop)**: Refers to the size of the lens opening, affecting the amount of light that enters and the depth of field.
        - **Wide Aperture (e.g., f/2.8)**: Allows more light; creates a shallow depth of field, perfect for portraits.
        - **Narrow Aperture (e.g., f/16)**: Allows less light; increases depth of field, ideal for landscapes.

2. **Adjusting ISO, Shutter Speed, and Aperture**

Manual Mode (M):

In **Manual Mode**, you have full control over ISO, shutter speed, and aperture.

1. **Switch to Manual Mode**:
    - Turn the **Mode dial** to **M**.
2. **Adjust ISO**:
    - Press the **ISO button** or access ISO settings via the menu.
    - Select the desired ISO value using the command dial.
3. **Adjust Shutter Speed**:
    - Rotate the **command dial** to set the shutter speed.

4. **Adjust Aperture**:
    - Hold the **exposure compensation button (+/-)** while rotating the **command dial** to adjust the aperture.

Program Mode (P):

In **Program Mode**, the camera sets the shutter speed and aperture automatically but allows you to adjust the ISO. You can override settings using the *Flexible Program (P)** feature.

- **How to use Flexible Program**:
    1. Rotate the **command dial** to shift between different combinations of aperture and shutter speed while maintaining the same exposure level.

Shutter Priority Mode (S):

- You set the **shutter speed**, and the camera adjusts the aperture automatically for proper exposure.
    1. Turn the **Mode dial** to **S**.
    2. Rotate the **command dial** to adjust the shutter speed.
    3. Adjust ISO manually if needed.

Aperture Priority Mode (A):

- You set the **aperture**, and the camera adjusts the shutter speed automatically for proper exposure.
    1. Turn the **Mode dial** to **A**.
    2. Hold the **exposure compensation button (+/-)** and rotate the **command dial** to adjust the aperture.
    3. Adjust ISO manually if needed.

3. Using Exposure Compensation

If you're using **semi-automatic modes (P, S, or A)**, you can adjust the brightness of your image by using **exposure compensation**.

1. Press the **exposure compensation button (+/-)**.
2. Rotate the **command dial** to increase (+) or decrease (-) the exposure.

4. Tips for Adjusting Exposure

1. **Balance ISO, Shutter Speed, and Aperture**:
    - Use a **low ISO** for bright conditions and increase it for low-light settings.
    - Match shutter speed to your subject (fast for action, slow for still scenes).
    - Choose an aperture based on depth of field requirements (wide for portraits, narrow for landscapes).

2. **Check the Exposure Meter**:
   - Use the **exposure indicator** on the screen or viewfinder to ensure your image is correctly exposed. Adjust settings until the indicator is near the centre.

3. **Use the Histogram**:
   - Check the **histogram** after taking a shot to ensure there are no extreme highlights (clipping) or shadows.

4. **Experiment with Manual Settings**:
   - Practice shooting in **Manual Mode** to better understand how ISO, shutter speed, and aperture work together to create the desired exposure.

5. **Use a Tripod for Long Exposures**:
   - For slow shutter speeds, use a tripod to avoid camera shake and ensure sharp results.

5. When to Adjust Exposure Settings

- **Bright Sunny Day**:
  - ISO: 100-200
  - Shutter Speed: Fast (1/1000s or higher)
  - Aperture: Narrow (f/11 to f/16)

- **Low Light/Night Photography**:
  - ISO: 800 or higher
  - Shutter Speed: Slow (1/10s or longer; use a tripod)
  - Aperture: Wide (f/2.8 to f/5.6)

- **Portraits**:
  - ISO: 100-400
  - Shutter Speed: Moderate (1/125s)
  - Aperture: Wide (f/2.8 to f/5.6)

- **Action Shots**:
  - ISO: 400-800
  - Shutter Speed: Very Fast (1/1000s or higher)
  - Aperture: Moderate (f/5.6 to f/8)

5.2 White Balance and Colour Options

White balance and colour options are essential for achieving accurate colours and creating the desired mood or style in your photos and videos. The Nikon P950 offers a range of white balance presets and colour customization tools to suit different lighting conditions and creative preferences.

1. What is White Balance?

White balance adjusts the camera's colour settings to compensate for the colour temperature of the light source, ensuring whites appear white and colours look natural.

- **Colour Temperature**:
    - **Warm Light (e.g., sunset, incandescent bulbs)**: Produces a yellow or orange cast.
    - **Cool Light (e.g., shade, fluorescent lights)**: Produces a bluish tint.

2. White Balance Presets

The P950 includes several white balance modes for common lighting scenarios:

1. **Auto White Balance (AWB)**:
    - Automatically adjusts to the lighting condition.
    - Ideal for most situations.
2. **Presets**:
    - **Daylight**: For sunny outdoor conditions.
    - **Cloudy**: Adds warmth to images taken under overcast skies.
    - **Shade**: Compensates for the cool tones in shaded areas.
    - **Incandescent**: Reduces yellow/orange tones from indoor light bulbs.
    - **Fluorescent**: Compensates for the greenish-blue cast from fluorescent lights.
    - **Flash**: Adjusts for the cool light from camera flash units.
3. **Manual/Custom (Preset Manual)**:
    - Allows you to manually set white balance by photographing a white or gray object under the lighting condition.
    - Best for mixed or unusual lighting conditions.
4. **Colour Temperature**:
    - Lets you select a specific Kelvin value to match the light source:
        - Warm tones: 3000–4000K
        - Neutral tones: 5000–6000K
        - Cool tones: 7000–10000K

3. Adjusting White Balance

1. **Accessing White Balance Settings**:
    - Press the **Menu button**.
    - Navigate to the **Shooting Menu**.
    - Select **White Balance** and choose the desired option.

2. **Quick Adjustment via Shortcut**:
    - Use the **Fn button** (if assigned to white balance) for quicker access.

3. **Using Manual/Custom White Balance**:
    - Select **Preset Manual** in the White Balance menu.
    - Point the camera at a white or gray object under the light source.
    - Press **OK** to measure and set white balance.

4. Colour Options

The Nikon P950 offers customizable colour settings to enhance or alter the appearance of your photos and videos.

1. **Picture Control**:
    - Adjusts the overall tone and colour of your images. Options include:
        - **Standard**: Balanced settings for general use.
        - **Neutral**: Minimal processing, suitable for post-editing.
        - **Vivid**: Enhances colour saturation and contrast.
        - **Monochrome**: Captures black-and-white images.
        - **Portrait**: Softens tones, ideal for skin tones.
        - **Landscape**: Boosts greens and blues for outdoor scenes.

2. **Adjusting Picture Control Settings**:
    - Access **Picture Control** from the **Shooting Menu**.
    - Select a preset and fine-tune parameters like sharpness, contrast, brightness, and saturation.

3. **Creative Effects**:
    - The camera also includes effects like **Sepia**, **High Key**, **Low Key**, and more for artistic expression.

5. Tips for White Balance and Colour Adjustments

1. **Use Auto White Balance for Mixed Lighting**:
    - AWB often handles mixed light sources well, but manual adjustments may be necessary for accuracy.

2. **Experiment with Picture Controls**:
    - Try different presets to see which matches your creative vision.

3. **Custom White Balance for Critical Colour Accuracy**:
    - Especially useful in product photography or scenes with unique lighting conditions.

4. **Combine Colour Options with Scene Modes**:
    - For beginner-friendly adjustments, pair the desired white balance setting with an appropriate **Scene Mode** (e.g., Portrait or Landscape).

5. **Shoot in RAW**:
    - If unsure about white balance, shoot in RAW format to adjust white balance during post-processing without degrading image quality.

5.3 Focus Settings (Manual and Autofocus)

The Nikon P950 offers both autofocus (AF) and manual focus (MF) options, providing flexibility to suit a variety of shooting situations. Mastering focus settings will ensure your subjects are sharp and your images meet your creative vision.

1. Autofocus (AF) Modes

Autofocus automatically adjusts the lens to focus on your subject. The P950 includes multiple AF modes for different scenarios:

AF Area Modes (Where the camera focuses):

1. **Face Detection**:
    - Detects and focuses on faces in the frame.
    - Ideal for portraits or group shots.

2. **Subject Tracking**:
    - Locks onto and follows a moving subject.
    - Great for action, wildlife, or kids.

3. **Target Finding AF**:
    - Automatically identifies the main subject and focuses on it.
    - Useful for general photography.

4. **Manual Select (Single Point)**:
   - Focuses on a specific point you select within the frame.
   - Ideal for precise compositions.
5. **Wide Area AF**:
   - Focuses on a larger area of the frame.
   - Suitable for landscapes or still scenes.
6. **Centre AF**:
   - Focuses on the centre of the frame.
   - Good for quick snapshots or when you plan to recompose the shot.

AF Modes (How the camera focuses):

1. **AF-S (Single AF)**:
   - Focuses once when the shutter button is half-pressed.
   - Best for stationary subjects (e.g., landscapes or portraits).
2. **AF-C (Continuous AF)**:
   - Continuously adjusts focus while the shutter button is half-pressed.
   - Ideal for moving subjects (e.g., sports or wildlife).
3. **AF-F (Full-time AF)**:
   - Continuously adjusts focus even without pressing the shutter button.
   - Useful for video recording or dynamic scenes.

2. Manual Focus (MF)

Manual focus lets you take complete control, allowing for precise adjustments that are especially useful in challenging conditions.

How to Enable Manual Focus:

1. **Switch to Manual Focus**:
   - Access the **Focus Mode** in the menu or use a dedicated button (depending on settings).
   - Select **MF** for manual focus.
2. **Adjust Focus**:
   - Use the **multi-selector dial** or **command dial** to fine-tune focus.
3. **Focus Assist Tools**:
   - **Focus Peaking**: Highlights edges of in-focus areas to assist with precision.
   - **Magnified View**: Zoom in on the LCD screen to check focus accuracy.

3. Switching Between Autofocus and Manual Focus

You can easily switch between AF and MF depending on the scenario:

- **Quick Switch**:
    - Assign a shortcut button (like the **Fn button**) to toggle between AF and MF.
    - Use the **focus ring** (if applicable) to instantly override autofocus.

4. Tips for Using Focus Settings

1. **Use Single Point AF for Precision**:
    - Select a specific focus point for portraits, macros, or any scene requiring accuracy.
2. **Enable Face Detection for Portraits**:
    - Automatically locks focus on your subject's face, ensuring clear results.
3. **Use Continuous AF for Moving Subjects**:
    - Combine **AF-C** with **Subject Tracking** for dynamic scenes like wildlife or sports.
4. **Switch to Manual Focus for Macros**:
    - Use MF for close-up shots, especially when autofocus struggles with small details.
5. **Utilize Focus Peaking for Manual Focus**:
    - Activate focus peaking for sharper, easier manual adjustments.
6. **Recompose with Center AF**:
    - Use **Center AF**, lock focus by half-pressing the shutter button, and then recompose your shot.
7. **Low Light Situations**:
    - Use **AF Assist Lamp** for better autofocus performance or switch to MF if autofocus struggles.

5. Common Scenarios and Recommended Focus Settings

Scenario	Recommended Focus Mode	AF Area Mode
Portraits	AF-S	Face Detection or Single Point
Sports/Action	AF-C	Subject Tracking
Landscapes	AF-S	Wide Area AF
Wildlife	AF-C	Subject Tracking
Macros	MF	N/A

Scenario	Recommended Focus Mode	AF Area Mode
Night Photography	AF-S or MF	Single Point

5.4 Metering Modes

Metering modes determine how your camera evaluates the light in a scene to set the proper exposure. The Nikon P950 provides several metering modes, each tailored to different shooting conditions. Understanding these modes helps you achieve well-exposed photos, even in challenging lighting.

1. Types of Metering Modes

a. Matrix Metering (Default)

- **What it does**:
    - Evaluates the entire frame, dividing it into multiple zones.
    - Considers the brightness, contrast, colors, and subject distance to calculate exposure.
- **Best for**:
    - General photography, including landscapes, portraits, and everyday shots.
- **Strengths**:
    - Produces balanced exposures, even in complex lighting.

b. Center-Weighted Metering

- **What it does**:
    - Focuses primarily on the centre of the frame while still considering the surrounding area.
    - Useful when the subject is in the middle of the composition.
- **Best for**:
    - Portraits or scenes where the subject occupies the centre of the frame.
- **Strengths**:
    - Effective for isolating the subject when the background is brighter or darker.

c. Spot Metering

- **What it does**:
    - Measures light from a small area around the selected focus point (approximately 2-4% of the frame).
    - Ignores the rest of the scene for exposure calculations.

- **Best for:**
  - High-contrast scenes where you need to expose for a specific part of the image (e.g., a backlit subject).
- **Strengths:**
  - Provides precise exposure for small areas.

d. Highlight-Weighted Metering

- **What it does:**
  - Focuses on preserving details in the brightest parts of the scene (highlights) to avoid overexposure.
- **Best for:**
  - Concerts, stage performances, or other scenes with bright highlights and dark shadows.
- **Strengths:**
  - Reduces the risk of clipping highlights in high-contrast lighting.

2. How to Change Metering Modes

1. **Via the Menu:**
   - Press the **Menu button**.
   - Navigate to the **Shooting Menu**.
   - Select **Metering Mode** and choose your preferred option.
2. **Quick Access:**
   - Assign metering mode to a customizable button (e.g., Fn button) for faster changes.

3. Choosing the Right Metering Mode

Scenario	Recommended Metering Mode
Landscapes	Matrix Metering
Portraits	Center-Weighted Metering
High-Contrast Backlit Subjects	Spot Metering
Concerts/Stage Lighting	Highlight-Weighted Metering
Close-Ups (Macro)	Spot Metering
Evenly Lit Scenes	Matrix Metering

4. **Tips for Effective Metering**

   1. **Matrix Metering for Most Situations**:
      - Start with matrix metering; it works well in diverse lighting conditions.
   2. **Use Spot Metering for Specific Subjects**:
      - Place the focus point on the subject to ensure proper exposure.
   3. **Bracket Your Shots**:
      - When unsure of the correct exposure, take multiple shots at different exposure settings.
   4. **Combine with Exposure Compensation**:
      - Adjust exposure compensation (+/-) to fine-tune the brightness after selecting a metering mode.
   5. **Be Mindful of High Contrast**:
      - Use highlight-weighted or spot metering to protect important details in bright or dark areas.
   6. **Review the Histogram**:
      - Check the histogram to ensure your exposure is balanced and no areas are overexposed or underexposed.

5.5 Using Bracketing

Bracketing is a powerful feature on the Nikon P950 that allows you to capture multiple shots of the same scene at different settings. This ensures you have a perfectly exposed photo or provides creative options to merge the images later. The P950 offers **Exposure Bracketing** as its primary bracketing tool.

1. What is Bracketing?

Bracketing automatically captures a sequence of shots where the camera adjusts a specific setting (e.g., exposure) for each photo. It's especially useful in:

- **Challenging lighting conditions**: Ensures proper exposure for bright and dark areas.
- **HDR photography**: Combine multiple exposures to create a high-dynamic-range (HDR) image.
- **Situations where precision is critical**: Like landscape or architectural photography.

2. Types of Bracketing on the P950

Exposure Bracketing (AE Bracketing)

- Automatically varies the exposure (brightness) across multiple shots.
- The camera adjusts the shutter speed or ISO while maintaining the same aperture.

3. Setting Up Bracketing

Step-by-Step Instructions:

1. **Access the Bracketing Menu**:
   - Press the **Menu button**.
   - Go to the **Shooting Menu**.
   - Select **Auto Bracketing** and choose **Exposure Bracketing**.

2. **Choose the Number of Shots**:
   - Options typically include 3 or 5 shots.
   - Example: For 3-shot bracketing, the camera will take one normal exposure, one underexposed, and one overexposed photo.

3. **Set the Exposure Increment**:
   - Choose how much exposure changes between shots.
   - Options: ±0.3, ±0.7, ±1.0, etc.
   - Example: At ±1.0, the camera will create photos 1 stop underexposed and 1 stop overexposed.

4. **Enable Bracketing**:
   - Bracketing will remain active until turned off.

5. **Take the Photos**:
   - Press the shutter button to capture the sequence.
   - Some settings require holding the shutter button until all bracketed shots are taken.

4. Practical Applications of Bracketing

a. High Dynamic Range (HDR)

- Merge bracketed images in post-processing to create an HDR image that preserves details in shadows and highlights.

b. Insurance for Proper Exposure

- Use bracketing when unsure about the correct exposure, ensuring at least one photo is properly exposed.

c. Creative Exposure Adjustments

- Experiment with underexposed and overexposed images for creative effects.

5. Tips for Using Bracketing Effectively

1. **Use a Tripod**:
   - Ensures alignment of bracketed shots, especially for HDR merging.

2. **Combine with Exposure Compensation**:
   - Adjust exposure compensation to shift the entire bracketing range (e.g., for very bright or dark scenes).

3. **Shoot in RAW Format**:
   - Provides more flexibility for editing bracketed photos.

4. **Check for Motion**:
   - Avoid bracketing with moving subjects, as differences between shots may create ghosting.

5. **Review Results**:
   - Use the LCD screen or histogram to verify the exposure range of your bracketed shots.

6. Recommended Settings for Common Scenarios

Scenario	Shots	Increment	Notes
Landscape Photography	3	±1.0 EV	For scenes with bright skies and dark shadows
HDR Creation	5	±0.7 EV	Capture more subtle differences in exposure
Low-Light Scenes	3	±0.7 EV	Ensure proper exposure without blown highlights
Challenging Lighting	3-5	±1.0 EV	Useful for indoor scenes with bright windows

CHAPTER SIX
VIDEO RECORDING

6.1 Video Modes and Resolutions

The Nikon P950 is equipped with advanced video recording capabilities, making it ideal for capturing high-quality footage. With a variety of resolutions and frame rates, it caters to different creative and technical needs, from casual shooting to professional video projects.

1. Available Video Modes and Resolutions

Resolution	Frame Rates	Notes
4K UHD (3840 x 2160)	30p, 25p	Best for high-resolution, cinematic videos.
Full HD (1920 x 1080)	60p, 50p, 30p, 25p	Smooth motion, ideal for action or slow-motion editing.
HD (1280 x 720)	60p, 50p, 30p, 25p	Good for smaller file sizes and online sharing.
VGA (640 x 480)	30p, 25p	Basic resolution, suitable for email or lightweight applications.

2. Choosing the Right Video Mode

- **4K UHD (3840 x 2160)**
    - Perfect for detailed footage and professional-grade videos.
    - Use when quality is a priority or for projects that require cropping in post-production.

- **Full HD (1920 x 1080)**
    - The most versatile option, offering a balance between quality and file size.
    - Ideal for YouTube content, vlogs, and action scenes.

- **HD (1280 x 720)**
    - Suitable for quick videos and situations where storage space is limited.
    - Great for online streaming or videos intended for social media.

- **VGA (640 x 480)**
    - Use for lightweight, casual projects where resolution is not a concern.
    - Suitable for low-bandwidth sharing or archiving.

3. **Adjusting Video Resolution and Frame Rate**
    1. **Access the Video Settings**:
        - Press the **Menu button**.
        - Navigate to the **Movie Settings** under the Shooting Menu.
    2. **Select Video Resolution**:
        - Choose from the available resolutions (e.g., 4K, Full HD, HD, or VGA).
    3. **Set Frame Rate**:
        - Select the desired frame rate (e.g., 60p for smooth motion or 30p for a standard cinematic look).
    4. **Enable Additional Features** (Optional):
        - Turn on **Wind Noise Reduction** or other audio settings for better sound quality.

4. **Special Video Modes**

a. **Time-Lapse Video**

- Automatically creates a time-lapse sequence.
- Ideal for capturing sunsets, traffic, or cloud movements.
- Accessible through the **Time-Lapse Movie** option in the Shooting Menu.

b. **Superlapse Movie**

- Captures fast-paced action by speeding up long recordings.
- Perfect for documenting events or travel footage in a short duration.

c. **Slow-Motion Video**

- Record at a high frame rate (e.g., 60p), then slow it down in post-processing for dramatic effects.

5. **Video Shooting Tips**
    1. **Use a Tripod**:
        - Stabilize the camera for smooth, professional-looking footage.
    2. **Experiment with Focus Modes**:
        - Use **Autofocus** for dynamic scenes or **Manual Focus** for precise control.
    3. **Monitor Audio**:
        - External microphones can improve sound quality compared to the built-in mic.
    4. **Pay Attention to Lighting**:
        - Ensure the scene is well-lit to reduce noise, especially in 4K.

5. **Consider File Size**:
    - Higher resolutions and frame rates require more storage. Use a high-capacity memory card.

6. Recommended Settings for Different Scenarios

Scenario	Resolution	Frame Rate	Notes
Cinematic Videos	4K UHD	30p	Captures high-quality, immersive visuals.
Action Scenes	Full HD	60p	Smooth motion for fast-moving subjects.
Social Media Clips	HD or Full HD	30p	Good balance of quality and file size.
Time-Lapse Photography	4K UHD or Full HD	30p	Ensures detailed and sharp results.
Casual, Quick Clips	HD or VGA	30p	Easy to share and store.

6.2 Using the Built-In Microphone

The Nikon P950 comes equipped with a built-in stereo microphone for capturing audio during video recording. While it's convenient and easy to use, understanding its features and limitations can help you make the most of it or decide when to use external audio solutions.

1. Features of the Built-In Microphone

- **Stereo Audio**: Captures sound from two channels for a more immersive audio experience.
- **Automatic Gain Control (AGC)**: Automatically adjusts the audio recording level to match the loudness of the environment.
- **Wind Noise Reduction**: Reduces distracting wind sounds during outdoor recording.

2. Adjusting Microphone Settings

Step-by-Step Instructions:

1. **Access Audio Settings**:
    - Press the **Menu button**.
    - Navigate to the **Shooting Menu**.
    - Select **Movie Settings** and then **Microphone Settings**.

2. **Set Microphone Sensitivity**:
    - Options: **Auto**, **High**, **Medium**, **Low**, or **Off**.

- **Auto**: Ideal for general use; adjusts sensitivity based on the environment.
- **High**: Use in quiet environments to amplify distant or subtle sounds.
- **Low**: Use in loud environments to prevent audio clipping.

3. **Enable Wind Noise Reduction**:
   - Select **Wind Noise Reduction** under the same menu.
   - Recommended for outdoor shooting in windy conditions.

4. **Test Audio Levels**:
   - Record a short video and play it back to check the audio quality and adjust settings as needed.

3. Tips for Better Audio Quality with the Built-In Microphone

1. **Position the Camera Thoughtfully**:
   - Keep the camera close to the subject to capture clear sound.
   - Avoid blocking the microphone openings with your hands or accessories.

2. **Minimize Background Noise**:
   - Choose quieter environments or isolate the subject from noisy surroundings.

3. **Use Wind Noise Reduction Outdoors**:
   - Turn this feature on to reduce distracting wind interference during outdoor recording.

4. **Avoid Handling Noise**:
   - Use a tripod or stabilizer to minimize noise from handling the camera.

5. **Monitor Audio with Playback**:
   - Review recorded videos to ensure the audio is clear and balanced.

4. Limitations of the Built-In Microphone

- **Lack of Directionality**:
  - Captures all ambient sounds, which may lead to unwanted background noise.

- **Sensitivity to Wind**:
  - Despite wind noise reduction, strong winds can still affect audio quality.

- **No External Monitoring**:
  - The P950 doesn't support headphones for real-time audio monitoring.

- **Basic Quality**:
  - While sufficient for casual recording, the built-in mic may not deliver professional-grade audio.

5. When to Consider an External Microphone

Unfortunately, the Nikon P950 does not have a microphone input jack. If high-quality audio is critical for your project:

- Use an **external audio recorder** (e.g., Zoom H1n or Tascam DR-05X) to capture sound separately.
- Sync the audio with your video during post-production using editing software.

6. Recommended Settings for Common Scenarios

Scenario	Microphone Sensitivity	Wind Noise Reduction	Notes
Indoor Recording	Medium	Off	Ensures clear audio with minimal background noise.
Outdoor Recording	Auto or Medium	On	Reduces wind interference effectively.
Quiet Settings	High	Off	Amplifies subtle sounds.
Loud Environments	Low	Off	Prevents distortion from loud sounds.

By using the built-in microphone effectively and understanding its limitations, you can ensure clear and balanced audio for your videos with the Nikon P950.

6.3 Adjusting Frame Rates

Frame rates determine how many frames are captured per second in a video, affecting the smoothness, motion style, and editing flexibility of your footage. The Nikon P950 offers a variety of frame rates for different creative and technical needs.

1. Available Frame Rates on the P950

Resolution	Frame Rates (fps)	Use Case
4K UHD (3840 x 2160)	30p, 25p	High-resolution cinematic or standard videos.
Full HD (1920 x 1080)	60p, 50p, 30p, 25p	Smooth motion for action or general video use.
HD (1280 x 720)	60p, 50p, 30p, 25p	Lightweight files for social media or casual use.
VGA (640 x 480)	30p, 25p	Basic resolution for lightweight, simple videos.

2. What Frame Rates Mean

- **30p (30 frames per second)**:
    - Standard for most videos, creating a natural, cinematic look.

- Ideal for general-purpose recording, such as interviews or tutorials.
- **25p**:
  - Common in regions using the PAL standard (e.g., Europe).
  - Use for compatibility with PAL video systems.
- **60p (60 frames per second)**:
  - Captures twice as many frames as 30p, resulting in smoother motion.
  - Best for fast-moving subjects, such as sports or wildlife.
  - Suitable for creating slow-motion footage in post-production.
- **50p**:
  - PAL equivalent of 60p, commonly used in PAL regions.

3. Adjusting Frame Rates on the Nikon P950

Step-by-Step Instructions:

1. **Access the Movie Settings**:
   - Press the **Menu button**.
   - Navigate to the **Shooting Menu**.
   - Select **Movie Settings**.
2. **Select Frame Size/Rate**:
   - Choose your desired resolution (e.g., 4K, Full HD, HD, or VGA).
   - Adjust the frame rate to match your needs (e.g., 30p, 60p).
3. **Confirm Your Selection**:
   - Once set, your selected frame rate will be used for all video recordings until you change it.

4. Tips for Choosing the Right Frame Rate

- **Smooth Motion**:
  - Use **60p or 50p** for sports, action, or wildlife footage to ensure smooth playback.
- **Cinematic Look**:
  - Choose **30p or 25p** for a more natural, movie-like appearance.
- **Slow-Motion Editing**:
  - Record at **60p** and slow it down in post-production for dramatic effects.
- **Storage Considerations**:

- o Higher frame rates (e.g., 60p) produce larger video files. Ensure you have a high-capacity memory card.
- **Regional Standards**:
    - o Use **30p/60p** in NTSC regions (e.g., the Americas, Japan).
    - o Use **25p/50p** in PAL regions (e.g., Europe, Africa).

5. Practical Scenarios for Frame Rate Selection

Scenario	Recommended Frame Rate	Resolution	Notes
Sports or Action Shots	60p	Full HD	Ensures smooth motion and sharp details.
Wildlife Videos	60p	Full HD or 4K	Great for capturing fast-moving animals.
Vlogs or Tutorials	30p	Full HD	Natural motion, ideal for general use.
Slow-Motion Clips	60p	Full HD or HD	Slow down in post-processing for dramatic effect.
Cinematic Projects	30p	4K UHD or Full HD	Movie-like appearance.
Casual Footage	30p or 25p	HD or Full HD	Balanced quality and smaller file sizes.

6. Things to Keep in Mind

- **Lighting Conditions**:
    - o Higher frame rates (e.g., 60p) may require better lighting to avoid dark or noisy footage.
- **Playback Device**:
    - o Ensure the playback device supports the selected frame rate for smooth viewing.
- **Editing Software**:
    - o If planning to edit your videos, choose a frame rate that is compatible with your software and project settings.
- **Storage and Battery Life**:
    - o Recording at higher frame rates consumes more storage and may drain your battery faster.

6.4 Time-Lapse Recording

The Nikon P950 includes a time-lapse recording feature that lets you capture dramatic sequences of slowly changing scenes, such as sunsets, clouds drifting across the sky, or bustling cityscapes. This feature creates a video by combining still images taken at preset intervals.

1. What Is Time-Lapse Recording?

Time-lapse recording condenses hours of real-world activity into a few seconds or minutes of video. This is done by capturing still images at regular intervals and playing them back at a faster frame rate.

2. Setting Up Time-Lapse Recording

Step-by-Step Instructions:

1. **Access Time-Lapse Mode**:
   - Press the **Menu button**.
   - Navigate to the **Shooting Menu**.
   - Scroll down and select **Time-Lapse Movie**.

2. **Select a Preset Scene or Custom Settings**:
   - The P950 offers predefined time-lapse modes for common scenarios:
     - **Cityscape**
     - **Landscape**
     - **Sunset**
     - **Night Sky**
   - Alternatively, choose **Custom** to set intervals and duration manually.

3. **Adjust Interval and Duration** (Custom Mode):
   - **Interval**: The time between each shot (e.g., 2 seconds, 5 seconds, etc.).
   - **Shooting Duration**: Total time for the time-lapse sequence (e.g., 10 minutes, 1 hour).
   - The camera calculates the resulting video length based on your settings.

4. **Set Exposure Settings**:
   - Use **Manual Mode (M)** for consistent exposure throughout the sequence.
   - Lock exposure settings if you're shooting a scene with changing light conditions, such as a sunset.

5. **Begin Recording**:
   - Position the camera on a stable tripod.
   - Press the **Shutter-Release button** to start recording.

3. Tips for Creating Stunning Time-Lapse Videos

1. **Use a Tripod**:
   - Stability is crucial for time-lapse photography. A slight movement can ruin the sequence.

2. **Plan Your Composition**:
   - Identify dynamic elements in the scene, like moving clouds, flowing traffic, or shifting shadows.

3. **Adjust Focus**:
   - Use manual focus to ensure the subject remains sharp throughout the sequence.

4. **Battery and Storage**:
   - Use a fully charged battery or an external power source, as time-lapse recording can drain the battery.
   - Insert a high-capacity memory card to accommodate the large number of shots.

5. **Monitor Weather and Lighting**:
   - Weather changes can enhance or disrupt your time-lapse. Check forecasts for outdoor shoots.

6. **Experiment with Intervals**:
   - Shorter intervals (e.g., 2 seconds) are ideal for fast-moving subjects.
   - Longer intervals (e.g., 10 seconds) work better for slow changes, like sunsets or plant growth.

4. Example Time-Lapse Settings

Scene	Interval	Duration	Resulting Video Length	Notes
Cloud Movement	5 seconds	30 minutes	12 seconds (at 25 fps)	Captures dynamic cloud patterns.
Sunset	10 seconds	1 hour	24 seconds (at 25 fps)	Great for transitions in lighting.
City Traffic	2 seconds	15 minutes	18 seconds (at 25 fps)	Captures busy urban activity.
Night Sky	20 seconds	4 hours	48 seconds (at 25 fps)	Perfect for star movement or Milky Way.

5. Editing Time-Lapse Videos

After recording a time-lapse, you can refine it in post-production:

- **Adjust Playback Speed**: Use editing software to change playback speed or create slow-motion effects.
- **Colour Grade**: Enhance the colours for a more dramatic look.
- **Stabilize Footage**: Apply stabilization tools to correct minor camera shakes.

6. Considerations for Time-Lapse Recording

- **File Size**:
    - Time-lapse videos can consume significant storage, especially at high resolutions like 4K.
- **Flickering**:
    - Sudden changes in exposure or white balance can cause flickering. Use manual settings to avoid this.
- **Battery Life**:
    - Consider an external power source for extended time-lapse sequences.

CHAPTER SEVEN
MENU NAVIGATION

7.1 Overview of the Menu System

The Nikon P950 features an intuitive and organized menu system that provides access to all its settings and features. Navigating the menu allows you to customize the camera for photography, videography, and playback, ensuring optimal performance in various scenarios.

1. Main Menu Categories

The menu system is divided into several categories for easy navigation:

Menu	Purpose
Shooting Menu	Adjust settings for photo and video shooting, such as image quality, ISO, and focus.
Playback Menu	Manage and edit your photos and videos, including delete, rotate, and retouch options.
Setup Menu	Configure general camera settings like date, time, display, and connectivity.
Network Menu	Set up Wi-Fi, Bluetooth, and other connectivity features.
Retouch Menu	Apply in-camera editing effects to your photos.
My Menu	Create a personalized menu with your most-used settings for quick access.

2. Navigating the Menu System

Accessing the Menu

1. Press the **Menu button** on the back of the camera.
2. Use the **Multi-Selector (arrow pad)** to navigate through menu categories and options.
3. Press the **OK button** to select a menu item.

Quick Tips for Navigation

- Use the **Zoom In/Out buttons** to quickly jump between sections.
- A green highlight indicates the currently selected option.

3. Detailed Overview of Each Menu

Shooting Menu

This menu provides control over all aspects of capturing images and videos.

- **Options Include**:
    - Image quality and size

- ISO sensitivity
- White balance
- Focus modes and areas
- Metering modes
- Time-lapse and interval timer settings

Playback Menu

Manage your captured content directly on the camera.

- **Options Include**:
    - View and delete photos/videos
    - Slide show playback
    - Protect images from accidental deletion
    - Retouch and edit photos (e.g., crop, straighten)

Setup Menu

Adjust fundamental camera settings.

- **Options Include**:
    - Date and time
    - Monitor/viewfinder brightness
    - Beep sounds and vibration settings
    - Firmware updates
    - Reset all settings to default

Network Menu

Manage the camera's connectivity features for sharing and remote control.

- **Options Include**:
    - Enable/disable Wi-Fi and Bluetooth
    - Pair with smart devices via the SnapBridge app
    - Configure wireless file transfer

Retouch Menu

Edit your images directly on the camera.

- **Options Include**:
    - Apply filters (e.g., monochrome, sepia)

- o   Red-eye correction
- o   Resize and crop
- o   Add effects like miniature or fisheye

My Menu

Customize a menu with your frequently used options for quick access.

- **Options Include**:
    - o   Add any setting from the other menus
    - o   Rearrange or remove items

4. Customizing the Menu System

1. **My Menu Customization**:
    - o   Navigate to **My Menu**.
    - o   Select **Add Items**.
    - o   Choose frequently used settings to add for quick access.
2. **Setting Defaults**:
    - o   If you're unsure of any changes, use the **Reset All Settings** option in the Setup Menu to return to factory defaults.

5. Tips for Efficient Menu Use

- **Familiarize Yourself with My Menu**:
    - o   Use this feature to avoid repeatedly searching for commonly used settings.
- **Use the Help Option**:
    - o   For detailed descriptions of menu items, press the **Help button (?)** when available.
- **Update Your Firmware**:
    - o   Periodically check for firmware updates in the Setup Menu to ensure access to the latest features and improvements.
- **Explore the Retouch Menu**:
    - o   For on-the-go editing, experiment with effects and corrections directly on the camera.

6. Practical Use of the Menu System

Scenario	Relevant Menu	Examples
Capturing in Low Light	Shooting Menu	Adjust ISO, shutter speed, and white balance.
Sharing Photos Wirelessly	Network Menu	Enable Wi-Fi and pair with your smartphone.

Scenario	Relevant Menu	Examples
Editing on the Fly	Retouch Menu	Crop or apply filters to your images.
Quick Access Needs	My Menu	Add frequently used settings like focus mode.
Troubleshooting	Setup Menu	Reset settings or update firmware.

7.2 Shooting Menu

The Shooting Menu on the Nikon P950 is where you manage all the settings related to taking photos and videos. This menu allows you to customize the image quality, focus settings, exposure, and more, to get the best results for different shooting scenarios. Below is an overview of the options available in the Shooting Menu.

1. Overview of the Shooting Menu Categories

The Shooting Menu is divided into several sections to keep everything organized:

Category	Description
Image Quality	Adjust the resolution and compression for photos.
ISO Sensitivity Settings	Set the camera's sensitivity to light.
White Balance	Adjust the color temperature of the image to match the lighting.
Focus Mode	Choose the method of focusing (autofocus, manual, etc.).
Metering	Choose how the camera measures light for exposure.
AF Area Mode	Select the area of the frame for autofocus to concentrate on.
Exposure Compensation	Manually adjust exposure for brighter or darker images.
Time-lapse/Interval Timer	Set up time-lapse or interval shooting for capturing slow changes over time.
Self-Timer	Set the camera to take a photo after a short delay, ideal for group photos.
Picture Control	Modify the color profile and style of your photos (e.g., vivid, monochrome).
Vibration Reduction (VR)	Turn on or off the camera's stabilization system to reduce blur from shakes.
Image Size & Quality	Adjust the size and quality of the image file.

2. Detailed Explanation of Each Option

Image Quality

- **File Format**:
    - **JPEG**: Compressed file format, smaller file size.
    - **RAW**: Uncompressed file format, gives more flexibility for editing.
- **Quality Settings**:
    - Choose between **Fine** (higher quality) or **Normal** (more compressed).

ISO Sensitivity Settings

- Adjust the camera's sensitivity to light.
- Options include **Auto ISO**, where the camera selects the best setting, or manually selecting ISO values (e.g., 100, 200, 400) for specific lighting conditions.
- Higher ISO values are useful for low-light situations but may introduce noise.

White Balance

- Adjusts the colour balance to match different lighting conditions.
    - **Auto White Balance (AWB)**: The camera automatically adjusts the white balance based on the scene.
    - **Manual White Balance**: You can choose a preset or set a custom white balance based on the lighting.
    - **Preset Options**: Daylight, Cloudy, Incandescent, Fluorescent, etc.

Focus Mode

- **AF-S (Single Autofocus)**: Focuses once when you press the shutter button halfway.
- **AF-C (Continuous Autofocus)**: Continuously adjusts focus as the subject moves.
- **Manual Focus (MF)**: You adjust the focus ring on the lens for precise control.

Metering

- **Matrix Metering**: Uses the entire frame to calculate exposure.
- **Centre-Weighted Metering**: Focuses on the centre of the frame for exposure calculation.
- **Spot Metering**: Measures exposure from a small spot in the centre of the frame.

AF Area Mode

- **Auto Area AF**: The camera automatically selects the focus area.
- **Single-Point AF**: Allows you to choose a specific focus point.
- **Dynamic-Area AF**: The camera uses a group of points around the selected point.

- **3D-Tracking AF**: Tracks a moving subject based on its initial focus point.

Exposure Compensation

- Adjusts the exposure if the image is too bright (overexposed) or too dark (underexposed).
- You can set it to a positive or negative value depending on the scene.

Time-lapse/Interval Timer

- Enables you to capture a series of images at set intervals to create a time-lapse video.
- **Settings**:
    - **Interval**: Time between each shot (e.g., 1 second, 5 seconds, etc.).
    - **Number of Shots**: Set how many shots the camera will take during the time-lapse.

Self-Timer

- Sets a delay before the camera takes a photo. This is ideal for group shots or selfies.
- Options include 2 seconds or 10 seconds.

Picture Control

- Adjusts the look of your photos with various presets:
    - **Standard**: Default colour settings.
    - **Vivid**: Increases saturation for more vibrant colours.
    - **Monochrome**: Black-and-white images.
    - **Neutral**: Softer colours with more natural tones.
    - **Portrait**: Optimized for skin tones.
    - **Landscape**: Enhances blues and greens.

Vibration Reduction (VR)

- **On/Off**: Turn the camera's vibration reduction feature on to stabilize handheld shots and reduce camera shake.

Image Size & Quality

- **Image Size**: Select the resolution (e.g., Large, Medium, Small) for photos.
- **Image Quality**: Choose between Fine (higher quality) or Normal (more compressed files).

3. Tips for Optimizing Your Settings

- **In Low-Light Conditions**: Increase ISO sensitivity, use a slower shutter speed, or enable VR for stabilization.
- **For Moving Subjects**: Set the focus mode to **AF-C** and choose **3D-Tracking AF** to track the subject.

- **Time-Lapse**: Use the **Interval Timer** setting to capture a series of photos at set intervals for creating stunning time-lapse videos.
- **Portrait Photography**: Use **Portrait** Picture Control for enhanced skin tones and **AF-S** for sharp focus on the subject.
- **Landscape Photography**: Use **Landscape** Picture Control and **AF-S** for sharp focus on distant objects.

4. Quick Access and Customization

You can create a personalized **My Menu** to save your favourite or frequently used settings from the Shooting Menu for faster access. This is useful when switching between different modes or settings during a shoot.

7.3 Custom Settings

The Custom Settings Menu on the Nikon P950 allows you to personalize various aspects of the camera's operation to better suit your shooting style and preferences. These settings can control everything from how the camera responds to your inputs, to specific behaviour like focusing and button assignments. Below is an overview of the options available in the Custom Settings menu.

1. Overview of the Custom Settings Categories

The **Custom Settings Menu** is organized into several sections for easy access:

Category	Description
Autofocus and Focus Area	Configure the autofocus behaviour, including focus mode and area settings.
Exposure and Metering	Adjust settings related to exposure control, such as bracketing and metering modes.
Button and Control Customization	Customize button assignments, control dial behaviour, and user interface preferences.
Display Options	Modify how information is displayed on the screen and viewfinder.
Flash Settings	Adjust settings related to the camera's built-in flash or external flash units.
Release and Shutter Settings	Control how the shutter responds to button presses, including release mode and focus.
File Management and Storage	Set options for file storage, file naming conventions, and card management.
Power and Battery Settings	Control battery-saving options, automatic power off, and other energy-related settings.

2. Detailed Explanation of Each Option

Autofocus and Focus Area

- **AF Area Mode**:
  - Set the autofocus to focus on a specific area (e.g., **Single Point**, **Dynamic Area**, **3D Tracking**).

- **AF Fine Tune**:
  - Calibrate the autofocus for specific lenses, useful for ensuring sharp focus on the subject.

- **Focus Mode**:
  - Choose between **AF-S (Single Autofocus)**, **AF-C (Continuous Autofocus)**, or **Manual Focus (MF)**.

- **Focus Tracking**:
  - Enable or disable focus tracking for moving subjects.

Exposure and Metering

- **Metering Mode**:
  - Select from **Matrix Metering**, **Centre-Weighted Metering**, or **Spot Metering** based on the scene's lighting.

- **Exposure Bracketing**:
  - Set the camera to automatically take several shots at different exposure levels (e.g., underexposed, correctly exposed, and overexposed) for HDR (High Dynamic Range) images.

- **ISO Sensitivity Settings**:
  - Control the camera's sensitivity to light, including setting Auto ISO or manual ISO adjustments.

Button and Control Customization

- **Custom Button Assignments**:
  - Assign specific functions to the buttons on the camera (e.g., assign ISO control to a customizable button for quick adjustments).

- **Control Dial Settings**:
  - Configure the behaviour of the control dials, including switching between aperture and shutter speed adjustments.

- **Function Button Settings**:
  - Customize the **Fn** button to perform actions such as toggling focus modes, activating HDR, or adjusting white balance.

Display Options
- **Info Display**:
    - Adjust what information appears on the screen and in the viewfinder, including grid lines, exposure information, battery level, and shooting settings.
- **Auto Review**:
    - Set whether the camera automatically displays an image preview after taking a shot and for how long.
- **Highlight Display**:
    - Enable or disable the feature that highlights overexposed areas of the image.

Flash Settings
- **Flash Mode**:
    - Choose from various flash modes such as **Auto**, **Fill Flash**, or **Slow Sync** depending on your lighting needs.
- **Flash Exposure Compensation**:
    - Adjust the power output of the flash for more or less light.
- **Red-eye Reduction**:
    - Enable red-eye reduction to avoid red-eye when using the flash.

Release and Shutter Settings
- **Shutter Release Priority**:
    - Decide whether the shutter button should prioritize focus or release, especially useful for continuous shooting.
- **Self-Timer Settings**:
    - Set the delay time for the self-timer (e.g., 2 seconds or 10 seconds).
- **Continuous Release Mode**:
    - Set the camera to take multiple shots in quick succession when the shutter button is pressed.

File Management and Storage
- **Image Quality Settings**:
    - Adjust the file format and resolution of the images (e.g., RAW, JPEG).
- **File Naming**:
    - Customize how files are named, such as adding a prefix or changing numbering formats.

- **Card Slot Priority**:
    - Choose which memory card slot the camera should prioritize when saving images.
- **Folder Management**:
    - Create and manage folders for organizing images on your memory cards.

Power and Battery Settings

- **Auto Power Off**:
    - Set how long the camera should wait before automatically turning off to save battery.
- **Battery Level Display**:
    - Display battery information on the screen to monitor usage.
- **Power Saving Options**:
    - Enable power-saving features like turning off the LCD screen when not in use.

3. Tips for Optimizing Your Custom Settings

- **Customize for Quick Access**:
    - Assign functions you use frequently to customizable buttons. For example, assign **ISO settings** or **White Balance** to the **Fn** button for quick adjustments.
- **Use Exposure Bracketing for HDR**:
    - Set up **Exposure Bracketing** to capture a range of exposures and later combine them for a high dynamic range (HDR) image.
- **Control Focus Precision**:
    - Use the **AF Fine Tune** option to ensure that your lens and camera autofocus are perfectly calibrated for sharp results, especially if using a zoom lens.
- **Optimize Power Management**:
    - Set the **Auto Power Off** function to conserve battery life when not in use. However, if you're shooting for extended periods, you may want to extend this setting for convenience.
- **Tailor the Info Display**:
    - Adjust the **Info Display** to show essential information only, such as ISO, aperture, shutter speed, and battery level, to avoid screen clutter.

4. Practical Use of Custom Settings

Scenario	Relevant Custom Setting	Examples
Quick Access to Settings	Custom Button Assignments	Assign ISO or white balance to the **Fn** button.

Scenario	Relevant Custom Setting	Examples
Shooting in Low Light	Exposure Bracketing, ISO Sensitivity	Use bracketing to ensure you capture the best exposure.
Maximize Battery Life	Auto Power Off, Power Saving Options	Set camera to turn off after a short period of inactivity.
Fast Action Shots	Continuous Release Mode, Shutter Priority	Enable continuous shooting mode for fast bursts.
Precise Focus	AF Fine Tune, Focus Mode	Fine-tune focus for your lens and use AF-C for moving subjects.

The Custom Settings Menu on the Nikon P950 is a powerful tool for tailoring the camera to your specific needs. With personalized settings, you can streamline your shooting process, enhance focus accuracy, and ensure that the camera works efficiently for your style.

CHAPTER EIGHT
PLAYBACK AND EDITING

8.1 Viewing Photos and Videos

To view photos and videos on the Nikon P950, you can use the camera's built-in playback features. Here's a comprehensive guide on how to view your captured media effectively:

Viewing Photos and Videos on Nikon P950

1. Accessing Playback Mode

- **Turn On the Camera**: Ensure your Nikon P950 is powered on.
- **Playback Button**: Press the **Playback button** (usually marked with a triangle icon) located on the back of the camera. This will switch the camera from shooting mode to playback mode.

2. Navigating Through Images

- **Use Multi-Selector**: Use the multi-selector (arrow keys) to scroll through your photos and videos. You can move left or right to view previous or next images.
- **Zoom In/Out**: To zoom in on an image for a closer look, press the zoom-in button (often marked with a magnifying glass icon). To zoom out, press the zoom-out button.

3. Viewing Videos

- When you select a video file in playback mode, press the **OK button** to start playback. You can pause and resume playback using the same button.
- While watching a video, you can also use the multi-selector to rewind or fast forward.

4. Copying Frames from Videos

- If you want to capture a still image from a video:
    - While playing back the video, press the **Menu button** and select the option to copy a frame as a still image.
    - Follow prompts to save this frame as a JPEG file.

5. Deleting Unwanted Files

- To delete photos or videos:
    - In playback mode, select the image or video you wish to delete.
    - Press the **Delete button** (usually marked with a trash can icon) and confirm your choice.

6. Protecting Images

- To prevent accidental deletion of important images:
    - Select an image in playback mode, press the **Menu button**, and choose the option to protect it.

7. Using HDMI Output

- If you want to view your photos and videos on a larger screen:
    - Connect your camera to an HDMI-compatible display using a micro HDMI cable.
    - Switch your TV or monitor input to HDMI, and you should be able to view your media directly from the camera.

8. Additional Playback Options

- The Nikon P950 also allows for basic editing functions in playback mode, such as trimming videos or rotating images.
- You can access these options through the menu while viewing an image or video.

By following these steps, you can easily view and manage your photos and videos on the Nikon P950, making it simple to review your work and share it with others.

8.2 Zooming and Cropping Images

The Nikon P950 offers impressive zoom capabilities and cropping options that enhance its versatility for various photography needs. Here's a detailed overview of how to utilize zooming and cropping effectively with this camera.

Zooming with the Nikon P950

Optical Zoom

- The P950 features an **83x optical zoom**, equivalent to a focal length range of **24mm to 2000mm** in 35mm terms. This extensive range allows photographers to capture wide landscapes as well as distant wildlife and subjects with remarkable detail.
- **Dynamic Fine Zoom**: This enhanced digital zoom effectively doubles the reach to **4000mm**, although it may result in some loss of image quality compared to using the optical zoom alone.

Zoom Controls

- **Rocker Switch**: The camera includes a rocker switch around the shutter button, which is pressure-sensitive. Pressing it gently allows for slow zooming, while pressing harder results in faster zooming. This feature is useful for achieving precise framing or quick adjustments when spotting fast-moving subjects.
- **Snap-back Zoom**: A dedicated button allows users to quickly retract the lens to find subjects that may have wandered out of frame. Holding this button will temporarily zoom out, making it easier to reframe your shot before returning to the previous zoom level upon release.

Zoom Memory Feature

- The P950 has a **Zoom Memory** function that allows users to set specific focal lengths for quick access. By selecting desired focal lengths in the menu, you can instantly jump to those settings when using the zoom rocker, which is particularly helpful in dynamic shooting environments like wildlife photography.

Cropping Images

In-Camera Cropping

- While the P950 does not have a dedicated cropping feature during shooting, you can achieve effective cropping during playback. When reviewing images, you can use the zoom function to magnify parts of an image for better focus assessment or composition review.

Post-Processing Cropping

- For more precise cropping, it's recommended to use photo editing software after transferring images to your computer. The RAW format (NRW) captures more detail and dynamic range, allowing for significant cropping without compromising image quality.

- Cropping in software like Adobe Lightroom or Photoshop can help refine compositions and focus on specific subjects within your images.

Considerations for Cropping

- Be mindful of resolution when cropping; while you can crop significantly from a high-resolution image, excessive cropping may lead to loss of detail.

- For wildlife photography or distant subjects, using the full optical zoom before capturing the image will provide more detail and allow for better post-processing options.

By understanding these zooming and cropping techniques, you can maximize the capabilities of your Nikon P950, ensuring you capture high-quality images whether you're photographing landscapes or wildlife from afar.

8.3 Deleting Files

To delete files on the Nikon P950, you can follow these steps to remove individual images or format the memory card. Here's a detailed guide:

Deleting Individual Images

1. **Access Playback Mode**:

    - Turn on your Nikon P950 and press the **Playback button** (usually marked with a triangle icon) to enter playback mode.

2. **Select the Image**:

    - Use the multi-selector (arrow keys) to navigate through your photos until you find the image you wish to delete.

3. **Delete the Image**:

    - Press the **Delete button** (often marked with a trash can icon). A confirmation dialog will appear on the screen.

    - Use the multi-selector to highlight **Yes**, then press the **OK button** to confirm deletion. The image will be permanently removed from your memory card.

Deleting Multiple Images

1. **Access Playback Mode**:
   - Enter playback mode by pressing the Playback button.

2. **Select Multiple Images**:
   - Navigate to an image you want to delete, then press the Delete button.
   - When prompted, select **Yes** to delete that image or choose the option for deleting multiple images if available.

3. **Use Group Deletion**:
   - If your camera is set to display images in groups (like continuous shooting sequences), you can select a group and choose to delete all images within that group at once.

Formatting the Memory Card

Formatting your memory card will erase all images and data stored on it. This is useful if you want to start fresh or if you're preparing the card for use in another device.

1. **Access Setup Menu**:
   - Turn on your camera and press the **Menu button**.
   - Navigate to the **Setup Menu** (indicated by a wrench icon).

2. **Select Format Card**:
   - Scroll down to find the option labeled **Format Memory Card**.
   - Select this option and confirm that you want to format the card. This action will permanently delete all files on it.

3. **Confirm Formatting**:
   - You will see a warning about formatting erasing all data. Highlight **Yes** and press the OK button to proceed.

Important Notes

- Deleting files does not completely erase them; they may still be recoverable with data recovery software unless formatted properly.
- Always ensure that you have backed up important images before formatting or deleting files.
- If you accidentally delete files, consider using recovery software as mentioned in some resources, although success can vary based on how much new data has been written since deletion.

By following these steps, you can effectively manage your photos and videos on the Nikon P950, ensuring that your storage remains organized and free of unwanted files.

8.4 Retouch Menu

The Retouch Menu on the Nikon P950 offers various in-camera editing options that allow users to enhance their photos without needing external software. Here's an overview of the features available in the Retouch Menu:

Retouch Menu Features

1. Crop

- This option allows you to select a portion of the image to keep while discarding the rest. It's useful for focusing on specific details or improving composition.

2. D-Lighting

- D-Lighting enhances details in shadows and highlights, making images appear more balanced and vibrant, especially useful for photos taken in challenging lighting conditions.

3. Filter Effects

- The camera provides several filter effects that can be applied to images, such as:
    - **Selective Colour**: Emphasizes specific colours while converting others to grayscale.
    - **Miniature Effect**: Creates a tilt-shift effect that makes scenes look like miniature models.
    - **Colour Sketch**: Gives a sketch-like appearance to photos.

4. Quick Retouch

- This feature automatically adjusts brightness and contrast to improve overall image quality with minimal user input.

5. Skin Softening

- This option smooths skin tones in portraits, reducing blemishes and imperfections for a more flattering appearance.

6. Small Picture

- Creates a smaller version of the original image, which is useful for sharing on social media or for email attachments.

7. In-Camera Movie Editing

- For videos, you can trim clips directly within the camera, allowing you to remove unwanted sections without needing to transfer files to a computer first.

How to Access the Retouch Menu

1. **Playback Mode**: Enter playback mode by pressing the Playback button.
2. **Select an Image**: Use the multi-selector to choose the image you want to edit.
3. **Open Menu**: Press the Menu button and navigate to the Retouch Menu.

4. **Choose an Option**: Select the desired retouching option and follow on-screen instructions to apply adjustments.

These retouching features make it easy for users to enhance their images directly on the Nikon P950, providing flexibility and creativity without needing additional software or devices.

CHAPTER NINE
CONNECTIVITY

9.1 Wi-Fi and Bluetooth Pairing

To pair your Nikon P950 camera with a smartphone using Wi-Fi and Bluetooth, follow these detailed steps:

Setting Up Bluetooth Connection

1. **Prepare Your Camera:**
   - Turn on your Nikon P950.
   - Navigate to the **Menu** and select the **Setup Menu** (wrench icon).
   - Look for the option labeled **Connect to Smart Device**. Ensure that Bluetooth is enabled and set to discoverable mode.

2. **Download SnapBridge:**
   - Install the **SnapBridge app** on your smartphone from the App Store or Google Play Store.

3. **Pairing Process:**
   - Open the SnapBridge app on your smartphone.
   - In the app, select **Add Camera** or tap the gear icon and choose **Pairing Bluetooth**.
   - The app should automatically detect your camera. Select it to initiate pairing.
   - Confirm any prompts on both your camera and smartphone to complete the pairing process. You may be asked to accept a Bluetooth pairing request on your phone

4. **Check Connection:**
   - Once connected, you can use SnapBridge to transfer images and utilize other features like GPS tagging.

Setting Up Wi-Fi Connection

1. **Enable Wi-Fi on Camera:**
   - In the same **Setup Menu**, look for **Wi-Fi Connection** and select it to enable Wi-Fi.

2. **Connect Smartphone to Camera's Wi-Fi:**
   - On your smartphone, go to the Wi-Fi settings.
   - Look for a network starting with "Nikon" followed by a series of letters and numbers, and connect to it.

3. **Using SnapBridge for Wi-Fi:**
   - After connecting to the camera's Wi-Fi, return to the SnapBridge app.

- Follow prompts in the app to establish a connection over Wi-Fi, which allows for faster data transfer, especially for larger files like RAW images or videos.

Troubleshooting Tips

- If you encounter issues:
    - Ensure that both Bluetooth and Wi-Fi are enabled on your camera.
    - Restart both your camera and smartphone.
    - Check that your camera is not in Airplane Mode, which disables wireless connections.
    - If connection options are not selectable in the menu, try switching the camera mode (e.g., from Aperture mode to Auto mode) as some users have found this resolves menu access issues.

By following these steps, you should be able to successfully pair your Nikon P950 with your smartphone via both Bluetooth and Wi-Fi, enhancing your photography experience with easy image transfers and remote control capabilities.

9.2 Using the SnapBridge App

Nikon's SnapBridge app enhances the photography experience by enabling seamless connectivity between Nikon cameras and smart devices. Here's a comprehensive guide on how to effectively use the SnapBridge app, including its features and setup process.

Overview of SnapBridge

SnapBridge allows users to:

- **Transfer Images**: Automatically transfer images from your camera to your smartphone as you take them. The app supports both JPEG and RAW formats.
- **Remote Control**: Use your smartphone as a remote control for your camera, adjusting settings like focus, aperture, and shutter speed.
- **Firmware Updates**: Receive notifications for firmware updates, allowing you to keep your camera up-to-date without needing a computer.
- **Cloud Storage**: Store images in NIKON IMAGE SPACE with up to 20 GB of space for 2-megapixel JPEGs.

Key Features

- **Automatic Transfers**: SnapBridge automatically saves a low-resolution version (2 MP) of each image taken, which can be easily shared on social media.
- **Camera Control**: Adjust settings remotely, including shooting modes (P/S/A/M), exposure compensation, and white balance. This feature is particularly useful for capturing images from difficult angles.
- **Easy Shooting Setup**: The latest versions include user-friendly setups for various shooting conditions, allowing users to save preferred settings for quick access.

Setting Up SnapBridge

Installation

1. **Download the App**: Install SnapBridge from the Google Play Store or Apple App Store.

2. **Check Compatibility**: Ensure your Nikon camera supports SnapBridge. Most recent models do, but it's good to confirm.

Pairing Your Camera

1. **Enable Bluetooth**: Turn on Bluetooth on both your camera and smartphone.

2. **Open SnapBridge**: Launch the app on your smartphone.

3. **Connect to Camera**:

    - On your camera, navigate to the menu and select "Connect to Smart Device."

    - Follow prompts on both devices to establish a connection. You may need to confirm pairing codes.

4. **Wi-Fi Connection** (if applicable): For models with Wi-Fi capabilities, connect your smartphone to the camera's Wi-Fi network after initial pairing.

Using SnapBridge

- Once connected, you can start transferring images and controlling your camera remotely. Explore the app's interface to access various features such as remote shooting and settings adjustments.

Troubleshooting Tips

- If you experience connection issues, ensure both devices have sufficient battery life and are within range.

- Restart both devices if necessary and check that Bluetooth is enabled on both ends.

By following these steps, you can maximize the functionality of your Nikon camera with the SnapBridge app, making it easier to share and manage your photography seamlessly.

9.3 Transferring Images to a Smartphone or PC

Transferring images from your Nikon P950 camera to a smartphone or PC can be accomplished through several methods, including using the SnapBridge app, a USB cable, or a memory card reader. Here's how to do each:

Transferring Images to a Smartphone Using SnapBridge

1. **Download the SnapBridge App**:

    - Install the SnapBridge app from the Google Play Store or Apple App Store.

2. **Pair Your Camera with Your Smartphone**:

    - Turn on your Nikon P950 and enable Bluetooth.

- Launch the SnapBridge app and follow the prompts to pair your smartphone with the camera. Make sure both devices display the same authentication code during pairing.

3. **Automatic Image Transfer**:
    - Once paired, SnapBridge can automatically transfer images from your camera to your smartphone as you take them. Ensure that your smartphone has Bluetooth enabled for continuous connectivity.
    - You can also browse and select images within the app for manual transfer if needed.

Transferring Images to a PC Using a USB Cable

1. **Connect Your Camera to PC**:
    - Use the supplied USB cable to connect your Nikon P950 to your computer.
    - Turn on the camera.

2. **Launch Transfer Software**:
    - Open Nikon's software such as ViewNX-i or Capture NX-D on your computer.
    - The software should recognize your camera. Follow the prompts to import images from the camera's memory card.

3. **Select and Transfer Images**:
    - In the software, you can select which images to transfer. Click "Start Transfer" after making your selections, and monitor the progress until completion.

Using a Memory Card Reader

1. **Remove Memory Card**:
    - Turn off your camera and remove the SD card from the Nikon P950.

2. **Insert Card into Reader**:
    - Insert the SD card into a compatible card reader connected to your PC.

3. **Access Files**:
    - Open File Explorer (Windows) or Finder (Mac) and navigate to the SD card. You can then copy and paste or drag and drop images to your desired location on your computer.

Additional Tips

- Ensure you have enough storage space on your smartphone or computer before transferring large files.
- For quicker transfers of high-resolution images, using a USB cable or memory card reader is generally more efficient than Bluetooth.
- Regularly check for updates for the SnapBridge app to ensure compatibility and access to new features.

By following these methods, you can easily manage and transfer your photos from the Nikon P950 to either a smartphone or PC, enhancing your workflow and sharing capabilities.

CHAPTER TEN
ACCESSORIES AND EXTERNAL FEATURES

10.1 External Flash and Hot Shoe

The Nikon P950 camera is equipped with a hot shoe that allows for the attachment of external flashes, enhancing your photography capabilities, especially in low-light conditions. Here's a detailed overview of using an external flash with the Nikon P950, including compatibility and functionality.

Hot Shoe and Flash Compatibility

Hot Shoe Features

- The Nikon P950 features an **ISO 518 hot shoe** that supports sync and data contacts, allowing for direct connection to compatible external flashes.

- This hot shoe enables the use of various Nikon Speedlights, which can provide advanced flash functionalities compared to the built-in flash.

Compatible External Flashes

The P950 is compatible with several Nikon Speedlight models. Recommended options include:

- **SB-5000**
- **SB-900**
- **SB-910**
- **SB-800**
- **SB-700**
- **SB-600**
- **SB-500**
- **SB-R200**
- **SB-400**
- **SB-300**

These flashes support features such as i-TTL (intelligent Through The Lens) flash control, which optimizes exposure automatically based on the scene being captured.

Using External Flash with the P950

Setting Up the Flash

1. **Attach the Flash**: Slide the external flash into the hot shoe until it clicks securely.
2. **Power On**: Turn on both the camera and the external flash.
3. **Select Flash Mode**: Depending on your shooting conditions, you may want to adjust settings on your flash for TTL, manual, or other modes.

Flash Control Options

The P950 allows for various flash control settings:

- **TTL Auto Flash**: Automatically adjusts flash output based on ambient light.

- **Flash Exposure Compensation**: Adjusts flash output in steps of 1/3 EV within a range of -2 to +2 EV.

These settings can be accessed through the camera's menu system, allowing for fine-tuning based on your shooting environment.

Considerations When Using External Flashes

- Ensure that your external flash is compatible with the P950 to utilize all available features effectively.

- Be aware that some advanced functions of newer Speedlights may not be fully supported by the P950; refer to the compatibility chart for specifics.

- For optimal performance, consider using flashes that support Nikon's Creative Lighting System (CLS), which enhances wireless control and multiple flash setups.

By utilizing an external flash with your Nikon P950, you can significantly improve your photography in challenging lighting situations, providing more creative control and versatility in your shots.

10.2 Using a Tripod

Using a tripod with your Nikon P950 can significantly enhance your photography, especially in low-light conditions or when capturing long exposures. Here's how to effectively use a tripod with the P950, including setup and benefits.

Benefits of Using a Tripod

- **Stability**: A tripod stabilizes the camera, reducing camera shake and allowing for sharper images, particularly at slower shutter speeds or when using telephoto zoom.

- **Long Exposures**: Ideal for night photography or capturing moving subjects (like waterfalls) where longer exposure times are necessary.

- **Composing Shots**: A tripod allows for precise composition adjustments and framing without the need to hold the camera, which is particularly useful for landscape photography.

Setting Up the Tripod with Nikon P950

Choosing the Right Tripod

- Ensure that your tripod has a **1/4-inch screw mount**, which is standard for most cameras, including the Nikon P950.

- Consider lightweight options for portability if you plan to travel or hike with your gear.

Attaching the Camera

1. **Mounting**: Align the camera's tripod socket (located at the bottom of the P950) with the tripod head and screw it securely into place.
2. **Leveling**: Adjust the tripod legs to achieve a stable and level position. Most tripods have adjustable legs that can be extended or shortened as needed.

Adjusting Settings for Tripod Use

- **Use a Remote Shutter Release**: To avoid any camera shake when pressing the shutter button, consider using a remote shutter release or the camera's self-timer feature.
- **Manual Mode**: Switch to manual mode (M) or aperture priority (A) to have full control over exposure settings. This is especially useful for long exposure shots.

Recommended Tripods

When selecting a tripod for your Nikon P950, consider options that provide good stability and portability:

- **Compact Tripods**: Lightweight models like those from brands such as Manfrotto or Gitzo are excellent for travel.
- **Ball Head Tripods**: Offer flexibility in adjusting angles quickly and easily, making them suitable for various shooting scenarios.

Additional Accessories

- **Tripod Head**: Depending on your shooting style, you may want to invest in a fluid head for video work or a ball head for quick adjustments in photography.
- **Weight Hook**: Some tripods come with a hook at the bottom of the center column where you can hang additional weight (like a camera bag) to improve stability in windy conditions.

By incorporating a tripod into your photography setup with the Nikon P950, you can achieve clearer images and explore creative techniques that require stability and precision.

10.3 Compatible Accessories

The Nikon P950 camera is compatible with a variety of accessories that enhance its functionality and improve the overall photography experience. Here's a comprehensive overview of compatible accessories for the Nikon P950:

Essential Accessories for Nikon P950

1. Batteries and Chargers

- **Replacement Batteries**: Ensure you have spare batteries, such as the EN-EL20a, for extended shooting sessions.
- **Battery Chargers**: The MH-29 battery charger is specifically designed for the P950, allowing you to charge your batteries efficiently.

2. Memory Cards

- **SD Memory Cards**: Use high-capacity SD cards (e.g., 64GB or 128GB) to store photos and videos. Look for UHS-I or UHS-II cards for faster write speeds, especially when shooting in RAW format.

3. Tripods and Monopods

- **Tripods**: A sturdy tripod is essential for long exposures and stable shots, particularly in low-light conditions.
- **Monopods**: For more mobility while still providing stability, consider using a monopod.

4. External Flashes

- **Speedlights**: Compatible external flashes like the Nikon SB-5000 or SB-700 enhance lighting control, especially in challenging lighting situations.

5. Filters

- **UV Filters**: Protect your lens from scratches and dust.
- **ND Filters**: Control exposure in bright conditions, allowing for longer shutter speeds without overexposing the image.

6. Lens Caps and Covers

- **Lens Caps**: Use Nikon LC series lens caps (e.g., LC-52) to protect the lens when not in use.
- **Hot Shoe Cover (BS-1)**: Protects the hot shoe from dust and damage when not in use.

7. Cleaning Kits

- **Sensor Cleaning Kits**: Essential for maintaining image quality by keeping the sensor clean.
- **Microfiber Cloths**: Useful for cleaning lenses and screens without scratching.

8. Camera Bags

- **Shoulder Bags or Backpacks**: Invest in a padded camera bag to safely transport your Nikon P950 along with its accessories.

9. Remote Shutter Releases

- Use a remote shutter release to minimize camera shake during long exposures or when taking self-portraits.

10. Software

- Consider software like Nikon Capture NX-D or ViewNX-i for photo editing and management.

These accessories are designed to enhance the versatility and performance of your Nikon P950, whether you are a casual photographer or a professional. Investing in quality accessories will help you make the most of your camera's capabilities and improve your photography experience overall.

CHAPTER ELEVEN
MAINTENANCE AND TROUBLESHOOTING

11.1 Cleaning the Camera and Lens

Cleaning your Nikon P950 camera and lens is essential for maintaining image quality and prolonging the life of your equipment. Here's a step-by-step guide on how to effectively clean both the camera body and the lens.

Cleaning the Camera Body

1. Gather Your Cleaning Supplies

- **Microfiber Cloth**: For wiping down surfaces without scratching.
- **Lens Blower**: To remove dust and debris without direct contact.
- **Q-Tips**: For reaching small crevices.
- **Isopropyl Alcohol** (optional): For disinfecting surfaces.

2. Exterior Cleaning

- **Turn Off the Camera**: Ensure the camera is powered off before cleaning.
- **Use a Lens Blower**: Gently blow away dust from the camera body, especially around buttons and dials.
- **Wipe with Microfiber Cloth**: Use a clean microfiber cloth to wipe down the body. Avoid using paper towels or rough fabrics that can scratch the surface.
- **Clean the Viewfinder**: If your P950 has a viewfinder, use a lens blower first, then gently clean with a microfiber cloth or a Q-tip wrapped in a lens cloth to remove smudges.

3. Sensor Cleaning (if necessary)

- **Manual Cleaning Mode**: If you notice dust spots in your images, you may need to clean the sensor. Refer to your manual for instructions on activating manual cleaning mode.
- **Use a Sensor Cleaning Kit**: If you decide to clean the sensor yourself, use a proper sensor cleaning kit designed for cameras. Avoid using Q-tips directly on the sensor.

Cleaning the Lens

1. Gather Lens Cleaning Supplies

- **Lens Blower**: To remove loose dust.
- **Microfiber Cloth**: For wiping the lens surface.
- **Lens Cleaning Solution**: Specifically formulated for optics (avoid household cleaners).

2. Initial Dust Removal

- **Use a Lens Blower**: Hold the lens facing down and gently blow air across the surface to dislodge any loose dust particles. This prevents scratching when wiping.

3. **Wipe with Microfiber Cloth**

- **Circular Motion**: Dampen a corner of the microfiber cloth with lens cleaning solution (if needed) and gently wipe the lens in circular motions. This method mimics how lenses are polished during manufacturing.

4. **Deep Clean (if necessary)**

- If there are stubborn spots, apply a few drops of lens cleaning solution directly onto the cloth (not on the lens) and repeat the circular motion cleaning process.

5. **Clean Both Sides of Filters**

- If you use filters on your lens, ensure you clean both sides using the same method as above.

Final Checks

After cleaning, inspect both the camera body and lens under good lighting to ensure no dust or smudges remain. Regular maintenance will help keep your Nikon P950 in optimal condition for capturing stunning images.By following these steps, you can maintain your camera's performance and image quality while ensuring that your Nikon P950 remains in excellent working order.

11.2 Error Messages and Solutions

The Nikon P950 may display various error messages that can be frustrating for users. Here's a summary of common error messages and their potential solutions.

Common Error Messages and Solutions

1. **"Battery Exhausted"**

- **Issue**: This message appears when the camera detects that the battery charge is low or empty.

- **Solutions**:

    - **Check Battery Type**: Ensure the correct battery type is selected in the camera's menu. Navigate to **Menu > Setup Menu > Battery Type** and confirm it matches your installed battery.

    - **Charging Procedure**: Follow the correct charging procedure. Plug the USB cable into the charger first, then into a wall outlet, and finally connect it to the camera while it is powered off.

Contact Cleaning: Clean the battery contacts on both the battery and inside the camera using isopropyl alcohol or a contact cleaner to remove any oxidation.

    - **Replace Battery**: If issues persist, consider replacing the battery, as it may be faulty even if new.

2. **"System Error"**

- **Issue**: This error indicates a malfunction within the camera's system.

- **Solutions**:

- **Remove and Reinsert Batteries**: Take out the batteries for a few minutes, then reinsert them and power on the camera.
- **Factory Reset**: Perform a factory reset by going to **Menu > Setup > Reset All Settings**. This can resolve software-related issues.

3. "Lens Error" or "Lens Retracting"

- **Issue**: This typically occurs when there is an obstruction or malfunction with the lens mechanism.
- **Solutions**:
    - **Check for Obstructions**: Inspect the lens area for any debris or obstructions that may prevent it from extending or retracting properly.
    - **Restart Camera**: Turn off the camera, remove the battery, wait a moment, then reinsert it and turn on again.

4. "Camera Not Recognized by Computer"

- **Issue**: The camera fails to connect when plugged into a computer.
- **Solutions**:
    - **Correct Memory Card**: Ensure a compatible Nikon-approved memory card is inserted in the camera before connecting.
    - **Check USB Connection**: Use a different USB port or cable if possible, as faulty connections can cause recognition issues.

5. "PTP I/O Error"

- **Issue**: Occurs during attempts to capture images via software like gphoto2.
- **Solutions**:
    - **Restart Camera and Software**: Turn off the camera, disconnect it, and restart both the camera and your computer software.
    - **Update Software/Firmware**: Ensure that both your camera firmware and any relevant software are up to date.

General Troubleshooting Tips

- Always ensure your camera is powered off before connecting or disconnecting cables.
- Regularly check for firmware updates from Nikon to fix bugs and improve performance.
- If problems persist after trying these solutions, consider consulting Nikon support or visiting an authorized service center for further assistance.

By following these guidelines, you can effectively troubleshoot common error messages on your Nikon P950 and maintain optimal functionality of your camera.

11.3 Resetting the Camera

To reset your Nikon P950 camera to its factory settings, follow these steps:

Resetting the Nikon P950

1. Power On the Camera

- Turn on your Nikon P950 by pressing the power button.

2. Access the Menu

- Press the **Menu** button on the back of the camera to open the menu system.

3. Navigate to Setup Menu

- Use the multi-selector or scroll wheel to navigate to the **Setup Menu** (indicated by a wrench icon).

4. Find Reset Option

- Scroll through the options until you find **Reset All Settings** or a similar option. This is typically located at the bottom of the setup menu.

5. Confirm Reset

- Select the reset option and confirm your choice when prompted. The camera will ask if you are sure you want to reset all settings to their default values. Choose **Yes** to proceed.

6. Complete the Reset

- After confirming, the camera will reset all settings to factory defaults. This process is quick and will restore all settings, including shooting modes and custom settings, back to their original state.

7. Optional: Format Memory Card

- If you intend to sell or give away your camera, consider formatting the memory card as well. This can be done from the setup menu by selecting **Format Memory Card** and confirming your choice.

By following these steps, you can successfully reset your Nikon P950, ensuring that all personal settings are cleared and the camera is returned to its original configuration. This is especially useful if you are troubleshooting issues or preparing the camera for a new user.

CHAPTER TWELVE
SPECIFICATION

12.1 Technical Specifications of Nikon P950

The Nikon P950 is a versatile bridge camera designed for both amateur and advanced photographers. Here are the detailed technical specifications:

Nikon P950 Technical Specifications

General

- **Body Type**: SLR-like (bridge)
- **Dimensions**: 140 x 110 x 150 mm (5.51 x 4.33 x 5.91 in)
- **Weight**: 1005 g (2.22 lb / 35.45 oz) including batteries

Image Sensor

- **Sensor Type**: CMOS
- **Sensor Size**: 1/2.3" (6.17 x 4.55 mm)
- **Total Pixels**: Approximately 16.79 million
- **Effective Pixels**: 16 million
- **Max Resolution**: 4608 x 3456 pixels

Lens

- **Lens Type**: NIKKOR lens with 83x optical zoom
- **Focal Length (Equivalent)**: 24–2000 mm in 35mm format
- **Aperture Range**: f/2.8–6.5
- **Minimum Focus Distance**: 1 cm (0.39 in)
- **Construction**: 16 elements in 12 groups (including ED and super ED elements)

Exposure and Shutter

- **Shutter Type**: Mechanical and CMOS electronic shutter
- **Shutter Speed Range**:
    - Mechanical: 1/4000 to 60 sec
    - Electronic: Up to 1/8000 sec
- **Exposure Modes**: Programmed auto, shutter-priority, aperture-priority, manual, exposure bracketing
- **ISO Range**: Auto, ISO 100–6400

Viewfinder and Display

- **Viewfinder Type**: Electronic viewfinder (EVF)
- **Viewfinder Resolution**: Approximately 2.36 million dots
- **LCD Screen Size**: 3.2 inches (8.1 cm) fully articulated
- **LCD Resolution**: Approximately 921,000 dots

Video Capabilities

- **Video Recording Format**: MPEG-4, H.264
- **Max Video Resolution**: 4K UHD at 30p or 25p
- **Microphone Input**: Yes (stereo)

Connectivity

- **Wireless Connectivity**: Wi-Fi and Bluetooth built-in
- **USB Port**: USB 2.0 (480 Mbit/sec)
- **HDMI Output**: Micro HDMI connector

Storage

- **Storage Types Supported**: SD/SDHC/SDXC memory cards

Battery

- **Battery Type**: Rechargeable Lithium-ion Battery Pack EN-EL20a

Other Features

- **Image Stabilization**: Dual Detect Optical VR (Vibration Reduction) effective up to 5.5 stops
- **Continuous Shooting Speed**: Up to 7 fps for up to 10 shots
- **Flash Options**: Built-in flash with external flash support via hot shoe

Price

- MSRP at launch was approximately $799.

These specifications highlight the Nikon P950's capabilities as a powerful compact camera suitable for a variety of photography needs, from wildlife and landscape photography to videography and more.

12.2 Supported File Formats

The Nikon P950 supports various file formats for both still images and video. Here are the supported file formats:

Supported File Formats

Still Images

- **JPEG**: Standard compressed image format widely used for photographs.
- **RAW (NRW)**: Nikon's proprietary RAW format that retains all image data, allowing for extensive post-processing without loss of quality.

Movies

- **MP4**: The video format used by the P950, which includes:
    - **Video Codec**: H.264/MPEG-4 AVC
    - **Audio Codec**: AAC stereo

File System Compliance

- The camera adheres to the **DCF** (Design Rule for Camera File System) and **Exif 2.31** standards, ensuring compatibility with various software and devices.

These formats allow users to capture high-quality images and videos while providing flexibility for editing and sharing.

THANK YOU FOR READING

www.ingramcontent.com/pod-product-compliance
Lightning Source LLC
Chambersburg PA
CBHW062111220526
45471CB00010B/3697